Making
Steampunk
Jewellery

NIKKI DRUCE

THE CROWOOD PRESS

First published in 2016 by
The Crowood Press Ltd
Ramsbury, Marlborough
Wiltshire SN8 2HR

www.crowood.com

British Library Cataloguing-in-Publication Data
A catalogue record for this book is available from the British Library.

ISBN 978 1 78500 214 4

Frontispiece: Seeking adventure

Acknowledgements
I would like to thank those that have helped me, through the kindness of their hearts, in creating this book: Becca and Sean at Twisted Pix Studios and Chilli Chapel, the beautiful model, who worked tirelessly on shooting, editing and producing some of the most beautiful photographs in the book. Katt Johnson for the loan of her DSLR camera – without you, there would have been no tutorial photos! My mum for sending me lots of helpful pieces of Victorian jewellery she had stashed away. My partner Neil for putting up with my moaning throughout the writing process and requests for chocolate and trips to the seaside. Kelly Marie Saunders for her help with Cosplay research. Tim Colivet for being my best friend and accompanying me on trips to the library when he'd much rather be doing something else and, finally, my two cats Newt and Daisy, who provided cuddles, headbutts and paper organization.

Dedication
This book is dedicated to my family, friends and my partner Neil but in particular my Gran, Vera Bennett, and my Mum, Avril Druce. Without you both I wouldn't have learned how to make plenty of somethings from a lot of nothings.

Typeset by Sharon Dainton.
Printed and bound in Malaysia by Times Offset (M) Sdn Bhd

Making
Steampunk
Jewellery

Contents

Introduction   7

1   Steampunk and its Origins   11
2   Materials and Equipment   21
3   Design and Mood Boards   27
4   Necklaces   31
5   Brooches, Rings and Pins   51
6   Headgear   61
7   Other Accessories   71
8   The Captain of the Airship   93
9   Putting an Outfit Together on the Cheap   111

Conclusion   121
Further Information   123
List of Suppliers   124
Index   126

Introduction

Jewellery is a timeless aesthetic. It's no wonder that you have probably had a few pieces of Granny's beloved jewels handed down to you or that you coveted the gorgeous gold-plated shell cameo that your great-grandmother used to wear. Have you ever found yourself staring in wonder through the window of a dusty antique shop at the glittering glass beads that sparkle in the light? Or perhaps rummaging to find the best pieces at the local jumble sale?

Jewellery is for the magpies of the world. It is for those who like to feel adorned and for those who know that the making of an outfit is down to the small touches and not the clothes themselves. Jewellery can be simple, understated, delicate and humble.

It can be grandiose and extravagant, sometimes opulent to the point of vulgarity.

In times where everyone is feeling the pinch, thrift and craft have become readily used buzzwords. Being able to make something yourself, however small or simple it may be, carries a new weight of pride. I found myself making jewellery and accessories for this very reason.

I was finding that I was spending an increasing amount of money on accessories instead of clothing, as it was a way of breathing a new lease of life into my wardrobe for a smaller amount of money. A simple t-shirt with a large necklace can make the t-shirt look brand new. So, with this in mind and having been inspired by video blogs, online craft forums and social networks, I decided to order a few supplies to get started.

When I first sat in front of my desk, I hit a wall. I had no idea what the fiddly bits to join jewellery together were called. I had to do some research and take time to learn a few basics before taking the leap. I ordered a basic kit online of what I thought I would need and sat down one night to start making. It was challenging and I truly had no idea what I was doing.

With a lot of mistakes, swearing and perspiring, my first necklace was made – a very simple chain with an antique-style fan charm on the end. I cannot describe the elation that followed once it was done. I felt as if I had won a battle!

I am, by nature, a very stubborn and determined character. I don't let things beat me easily. I felt that I had won this time and it left me wanting to try more projects.

So with my recent crafty conquest under my belt and after considering the type of jewellery I wanted to make, I started to think about the jewellery I really liked to wear. I have always been fascinated with miniatures, making dioramas and small dolls house food and furniture: a theme I still appropriate in some of my current work. This led me to think about designs that would allow me to create dioramas suspended in time. I ordered some crystal clear resin, did a lot more research into how best to work with the material, and started making resin pendants. I discovered that using silicone moulds was the easiest and simplest way to form the resin.

I came up against a wall when trying to figure out how to attach the jump rings onto the pendants. Placing them into the resin made them sink, gluing them onto the pieces often led to them falling off, and drilling through the pendants led to the pendants cracking and breaking. So eventually, after even more research, I discovered glue-on bails and strong jewellery adhesive, which made it incredibly simple and quick for me to finish the pendants to a high standard. Without this period of

LEFT: Necklace design by Devine Delinquents. (Charis Talbot Photography)

Necklace design by Devine Delinquents.

Introduction

learning and trial and error, I wouldn't have developed the skills I have today. I am now an accomplished maker because I took the time to try things out and enjoyed the experience of them failing, even though it was frustrating at the time.

Resin is a very difficult medium to use, and I'm not afraid to tell you that there were a few accidents and a lot of wasted product. However, I look back at that time now and see it as a very valuable learning experience. I grabbed hold of the technique and ran with it, not afraid to try out all manner of experimental techniques to achieve the results I was looking for.

Looking back, perhaps a potentially dangerous substance was not the best thing to start learning with, but it helped to shape my future in jewellery design and I had to learn fast or give up – and I won't let myself quit! Eventually the time came when I grew out of resin. I decided that the process was too time-consuming and it was time to find something more suited to the amount of time I had to dedicate to jewellery-making. At this point I was still running my jewellery business alongside a full-time job. All my spare time was taken up with discovering my new craft, and most evenings and weekends were spent sweating or freezing in a poorly insulated garage which doubled as my workshop.

I continued to branch out into simpler forms of design and I found that the more fluid the design was, the better it was received by friends and the more

timeless and versatile the creation was. At this time, I didn't have a customer base and I started to explore niche markets. I have always been drawn to alternative culture since my early teens, so it felt natural to delve into that realm as it was something I knew about. I started researching into goth, punk, rock and any culture that had a strong musical influence. I then stumbled across Steampunk.

Steampunk is a genre that's out on its own as it doesn't really have a heavy musical influence – more of an influence from the love of comics, sci-fi, Victoriana and all-round geekery. It appealed to me as it has a wonderful sense of community and a unique expressionism that I could really sink my teeth into. I began making a few Steampunk-inspired pieces, arranging photoshoots with models to showcase and market them. I found that people really liked my designs so my shop, Devine Delinquents, was created and I've not looked back since.

When someone asks where you got your necklace, brooch, bracelet or fascinator from, 'Oh, this? I made it myself' has to be one of the most satisfying responses that can ever tumble from your lips. The more compliments you receive on your handmade items, the more you will feel inspired to try your newly learnt techniques and begin exploring the craft of jewellery-making.

However you like to wear your jewellery and accessories, there will be a

project in this book which can be adapted to your own personal style. You will learn how to use techniques and methods to create your own items of Steampunk-inspired jewellery through a variety of projects.

The book is set out as a series of projects, which are written in a step-by-step format to make them easy to follow and easy to progress through. Some projects are simple and will take under an hour to make; others are more complex and, depending on how intricate you'd like to make your items, may take you a few days to complete.

Each project lists all the items and materials you need, covers all the necessary steps, and guides you gently through those first important steps into the creative realm. Some of you will already be accomplished crafters and makers, but I hope that even in some of these basic projects there will be a few tips you can pick up. The more difficult projects will require some of the skills learnt in the easier projects, and I advise you to have a quick glance through each project to begin with and familiarize yourself with some of the techniques.

Good luck, and don't get disheartened if things don't work for you the first time. The best advice I can give you is to make it fun. If you stop having fun, put down the pliers and step away. You want your project to be infused with the right energy and an angry hat does not make for a pretty hat! Having said that, persevere and don't let yourself be beaten.

Chapter 1
Steampunk and its Origins

It is possible to believe that all the past is but the beginning of a beginning, and that all that is and has been is but the twilight of the dawn. It is possible to believe that all the human mind has ever accomplished is but the dream before the awakening.
– H.G. WELLS

'Steampunk' was first used as a term in 1987. This genre-busting movement encompasses many different elements, its main focus being Victoriana and steam-powered, post-apocalyptic machinery. The love affair with Victorian fashions has produced opulent and extravagant designs and has created some of the most innovative fashions of the 21st century. Steampunk was born from an evolution of style. It has been coined as 'Goths growing up' and 'Goths discovering the colour brown'. I feel this is unfair, as Steampunk is an amalgamation of fashions but also a style of its own. Steampunk's new influences hail from the worlds of comics, cosplay, computer games and other forms of affectionate obsessive geekery. The form and fashion of Steampunk has elements of the form-fitting Victorian style – corsets, bustles, maxi hooped skirts and intricate extravagant jewellery and millinery – but also encompasses the rag-tag style of post-apocalyptic survivors in a fantasized war-torn, ravaged world.

Steampunk is effectively the reimagining of the Victorian era in a dreamworld, where the past developed in such a way that the world evolved into a post-apocalyptic, steam-powered landscape of adventurers and explorers riding around in airships and shooting ray guns at invading aliens from different worlds. If the world was wiped out and we had to start all over again, chances are that starting from scratch would mean we would need to utilize our resources differently and think about things in basic terms, and this makes for an interesting topic and a great theme to build a movement around.

Post-apocalyptic fashion saw an emergence in the mid to late 1980s, perhaps as a backlash to the economic boom, and this was mirrored by a handful of films at the time which featured post-apocalyptic themes. The amalgamation of the two genres – the post-apocalyptic and the Victorian – didn't really happen until the late Eighties when a few sci-fi authors began writing stories influenced by the Victorian era with futuristic post-apocalyptic elements. The term was coined by an author trying to describe the stories he had been reading.

Before Steampunk gained its name, it was often confused with Retrofuturism, a movement within design that is focused on depictions of an idealistic utopian future dreamt up in the past.

Retrofuturism is often combined with Steampunk to create an overall style, but the two are quite different. Retrofuturism tends to lean more towards the retro side of styling rather than the future element; think of space-age sci-fi from the 1960s as a base point. Retrofuturism as an established term came about around the same time as the Steampunk term was coined, in the late 1980s. However, the style itself can be seen in plenty of films and television programmes before this time, from the 1960s onwards. The style evolved mainly during the space race years with authors, artists, filmmakers and designers jumping on board with all things sci-fi, metallic and rocket ship shaped.

Steampunk was more concerned with the dull gold hue of mechanical Victorian engineering, large heavy industrial machines and plenty of gear grease. This made the style evolve into something altogether more focused on the Victorian era, with a small touch of futurism thrown in. This may be because the era was more visually intricate and provides a recognizable reference point for people to latch onto or perhaps because the romanticism of the period

Example of a Dreampunk look by Nikki Druce, wearing a Devine Delinquents headpiece.

shines through. Whatever it is, it has made Steampunk instantly recognizable and allowed the genre to form into a strong fashion trend.

Steampunk has many sub-genres and these can be seen in a multitude of different places. Some sub-genres of Steampunk include Dieselpunk, Dreampunk and Decopunk.

Dieselpunk features darker colours, muted tones and is more gothic-influenced than the other sub-genres. For Dieselpunk inspiration within pop culture, look at computer games such as *Bioshock* and the film *Suckerpunch*, both of which contain strong Dieselpunk styles. Other films and games that feature references to Dieselpunk are the new *Batman* films and games, *Mad Max: Fury Road, Iron Sky* and *Sky Captain And The World Of Tomorrow*. All these films and games feature stylized Dieselpunk elements which can be great to draw inspiration from, particularly if you want to make items that are in a darker vein than the brighter, cleaner Steampunk.

Dreampunk is a fashion trend that has a take on dreamlike literature but still includes some Steampunk elements. Think of *Alice in Wonderland* with a ray gun and you'll get the idea! Dreampunk is a relatively new sub-genre which is still finding its feet, so it is a good theme to explore as there are currently no hard and fast rules. There are quite a few online forums dedicated to it where you can converse with other people who are interested in this style. Dreampunk also has links with fantasy and fairytales and can be teamed with themes from those genres to create something beautiful, soft and dreamy but with a harder industrial edge.

Decopunk is inspired by the modern sleekness of the 1920s through to the 1950s. It is a style that encompasses fully polished looks that don't have a hair out of place. It is the antithesis of

Dieselpunk, being smooth, clean and chrome in appearance. Decopunk takes its inspiration from the art of the 1920s, architecture from the period and also mainstream fashion of the time. Fashion from films and books like *The Great Gatsby*, *Metropolis* and *Midnight in Paris* borrow heavily from the Art Deco period and have some wonderful sequences that should provide you with many ideas to translate into your own designs. Take inspiration from places such as the Paris Metro, too, which has some of the best Art Nouveau architecture in the world.

Don't be afraid to combine Steampunk sub-genres like Decopunk and Dieselpunk together, as you may create something wonderful. You could always try to invent your own sub-genre within Steampunk and use your ideas to create something new. There is plenty of inspiration around to provide you with an untapped source of ideas which you can use to your advantage.

Victorian Jewellery

Certain things spring to mind in relation to Steampunk: corsets, cogs, opulent colours and most importantly the Victorian era. On discovering Steampunk and looking closely at the genre and its influences, I began to delve deeper into my love of Victorian jewellery. Researching and comparing the types of jewellery that were popular at that time led me to think about how the designs were created and by whom. I compared them with the popular items I had seen in modern designs or that I had been requested to design for customers in the Steampunk style.

The few elements that have stood the test of time are the pieces that hold memories and are timeless. Lockets, religion-inspired pieces and birthstones are all very popular as decorative trinkets and as personal items worn close against the skin. It is no coincidence that these elements of design were also a popular recurring theme in Victorian jewellery-making. Jewellers were regularly requested to make personal keepsakes, and were able to earn a living wage by doing so.

During the Victorian era family members were regularly sent away to work and were absent from home on a regular basis, and the mortality rate was depressingly high. People found they needed items to remind them of loved ones when they were away or if they had died. Photography was not available to all as it is now, and a keepsake such as a carved piece of jet or a hand-painted cameo was the best way of remembering someone. The explosion in sentimental jewellery in the mid to late Victorian period came about due to public demand. Sentimental jewellery was born to accommodate the need by Victorians to commemorate almost every event and occasion. Pieces were made for communions, weddings, funerals, birthdays, wedding anniversaries and in memory of pets, amongst other things.

The romanticism of the Victorian era can best be described by a story about Queen Victoria herself. After her beloved husband Albert passed away in 1861, Victoria went into an extensive period of mourning and didn't appear in public for a number of years. Her extensive collection of *memento moris* consisted mainly of pieces made of Whitby jet, a gemstone of a solid black colour that could be carved into many intricate and elaborate designs. The demand for jet went through the roof and many jobs were created to mine for the gemstone and to create beautiful designs from it.

Jet was reserved for the more affluent members of society, although others tried to copy it in a more affordable way using other types of material. Bog wood and base metals used for mounting pieces made items more accessible to the masses and the popularity boomed. The fascination with all things jet quickly dissipated and after the 1920s became close to non-existent. In recent years, however, jet has seen a revival and

My collection of Victorian and turn-of-the-century jewellery.

is now highly revered for more than its ties to the Victorian period and its morbid connotations. There are still craftsmen who produce hand-carved items made of jet as well as collectors of modern-day pieces, but most people interested in the gemstone today will pick pieces from the Victorian period when it was at its heyday and the craftsmanship was second to none.

The Victorians also liked semi-precious stones in their jewellery, as well as natural elements such as carved shells, bone, teeth and fur. Cut or engraved glass was to become more popular towards the end of the period as techniques improved, but many different materials were used and jewellery was often made from found items and objects that were readily available.

Motifs and designs for Victorian jewellery were incredibly varied, probably due to the fact that all jewellery was handmade. Jewellery was either made by those who would be wearing it, or else pieces were commissioned with personal ideas and designs in mind. This meant that items were not mass-produced and designs stayed relatively unique.

Some jewellery motifs become popular because of certain connotations. For example, religious iconography, floral designs and certain animals are all well used designs because of their personal meaning to individuals. The Victorians also knew how to think outside the box when it came to designing jewellery and often created designs based on things that may not seem important to us now but were incredibly treasured memories at the time. Whole collections of jewellery were made around holidays taken in the UK by one wealthy family, others took teeth from deceased pets to turn into trinkets, and some collected hair from loved ones to weave into intricate designs. No design was too outlandish for the Victorians, and the stranger the better.

To get some inspiration for your own Steampunk creations, try looking at Victorian jewellery online, in museums or in books. This should give you some interesting ideas to work with and help you create some unique pieces.

Gothic Sensibilities

Romanticism, beauty and a touch of darkness: how Steampunk became brooding

Steampunk has an air of romanticism that has most definitely been borrowed from the gothic genre of fashion. A lot of people interested in Steampunk have moved on naturally from the gothic side of alternative culture and have found themselves wanting to express themselves a little more with colours and styling. Gothic culture has a fairly strict set of rules, and Steampunk is a little more free-flowing when it comes to fashion. This makes it appealing to many different people, and as it is slightly softer looking and can be applied to a number of looks it has the ability to be more versatile and easier to fit into a day-to-day look. For a lot of people the gothic look is a little harsh and its exclusive use of the colour black can be a little heavy for some palettes and too restrictive.

A casual Steampunk look could be worn to the office, whereas a gothic look may be too bold. Steampunk can be mixed with a lot of other styles to make it lighter, and has managed to merge into many different genres, and into the mainstream in some cases. It also reaches into the fantasy, faerie world, with sub-genres popping up like Mori Girls, a nature-inspired version of Steampunk. Steampunk has also crossed into more serious haute couture fashion, with high-end designers embracing its futuristic influence. Occasionally Steampunk-inspired clothing will also pop up on the high street and be easy to find, making it simple and fairly inexpensive to get a pre-made item.

Gothic clothing is the same and can be found quite readily on the high street. However, it is important to stay away from items that are more cartoony. For example, anything containing too many skulls, bats or spiders can look too childish if not executed well. That's not to say that you should veer away from any of these motifs, but use them sparingly. Combining the two styles does make for a very striking look and is more in the vein of Dieselpunk, a Steampunk sub-genre.

The versatility of Steampunk and its strong themes make it very easy to borrow elements from and to transpose them into other styles and everyday wear. This may be one of the reasons that Steampunk has become so recognizable in recent years. Elements from the genre appear in all manner of places from modern pop videos to fashion magazines. At first, these versions may not be instantly recognizable as Steampunk, but once you have become *au fait* with the various elements, you will see the influence in many different places.

When Steampunk is referenced in today's pop culture, it is quite often used as a clunky metaphor for the technological revolution that we are currently experiencing. When Steampunk first came about and was in its infancy, things were starting to change within technology and modern culture. The internet was evolving into something that was becoming more popular in homes, phones were becoming mobile, television was gaining more channels, and programming was becoming more documentary- and reality-based. In today's society, Steampunk is used as a way of reminding us of our developing world and serves as a good reminder to

Gothic styled look by Charis Talbot Photography, jewellery by Devine Delinquents.

pay attention to our relationship with technology.

Steampunk has found itself emerging from the gothic scene and has raised its head above the parapet to be embraced by those who seek a touch of romanticism with their darkness. The idea of a post-apocalyptic world and a rebuilding of society lends itself to a romantic ideal, in such a way that there is always a romantic coupling in every end of the world movie or in every book on the same theme. It's worked for so many years that the formula doesn't need to be rewritten.

The Victorians were hopeless romantics and they had great gothic sensibilities when it came to fashion, literature, architecture and even the tragedies of that time. Mysteries and legends were forged around such macabre things as murders and the supernatural. Jack the Ripper, for example, was reported as being something of a notorious cad who preyed upon helpless female victims, something that the people of the time were sickeningly interested in and even heralded. Unspeakable crimes were committed and yet people found themselves engrossed in the terror and tragedy that surrounded them.

The Victorians were also obsessed with trying to contact the dead, and spiritualism became something of a parlour trick for some families. The ouija board, as we know it today, was patented in the Victorian period and the people of the time became fascinated with talking to the dead. Spiritualism offered a romanticized view of death and gave it a voice to speak with those still living. As a result the draw to gothic sensibility became heightened during this time, which led to mourning jewellery becoming more popular.

The Victorians had an unhealthy obsession with death: families were expected to go through months and years of mourning when a loved one passed, and Queen Victoria herself lived through an extended mourning period. This, linked with a high mortality rate brought on by various incurable diseases of the time, poor quality of life and general poverty, made for a macabre yet intriguing historical period. Steampunk has grown apart from the original gothic leanings attributed to the Victorians and become more of a fantasized modern version of that period. You still see Steampunk referencing a lot of Victorian funereal elements such as veils, layered bustles, cameos and top hats. However, the shades of black are usually replaced by other hues from the Steampunk colour palette, such as gold, beige and burgundy.

Comics, Cosplay and Computer Games

Steampunk's main inspirations and the modern twist

Steampunk has evolved in the twenty first century through the mediums of comics, cosplay and computer games. The glistening gold and machinery have proved popular topics for modern writers and many new works of fiction and creativity have featured the fascinating fantasy world of Steampunk. As there are no hard and fast rules for Steampunk and as it is a multi-faceted genre, there is a plethora of topics that can be covered with grandiose, bleak apocalyptic or even nature-based backgrounds. Most Steampunk-inspired stories have one or two things in common: the underdog makes good against a bigger force, or a revolution-inspired battle takes place. A large proportion of writers borrow from authors of the actual period like H.G. Wells or Jules Verne, taking their terms and ideology and then putting a modern twist on it. Both Verne and Wells were the grandfathers of idealized futurology

and speculative science fiction writing and this was adopted by authors and creatives in the late 1980s and early '90s.

Many comics have Steampunk as the main theme. Steampunk is perfect for graphic novels as it is able to provide storylines linked to adventure and the classicism of the Victorian era, which fit well when given a manga makeover. Steampunk fashion inspiration can be drawn from comics, as quite often the lead characters are imagined wearing fanciful and interesting creations. These elements can be taken from the page and recreated within your own wardrobe. Browsing through Steampunk comics may inspire you to create items based on those characters you encounter, but be mindful not to copy outfits photographically unless you are creating a cosplay outfit.

Take inspiration from characters in comics and pick out small details you may notice. For example, some female characters have excellent hairstyles, which can be partially emulated or deconstructed to suit your own hair. Male characters may have a certain design of goggle that you find interesting. Don't be bound by the gender specifics of characters either. If you like an element of a drawing you encounter, note it down or add it to a mood board to reference later. Reading Steampunk comics may also give you ideas about jewellery you may wish to create. Certain storylines may spark ideas and these should all be noted down along the way to help the creative process later on.

The Steampunk movement within fashion has only really been popular in the last few years. This could be a direct result of people transforming the look into cosplay styles, which invariably transcends onto the catwalk or into the mainstream after a certain amount of dilution to make it more palatable to a wider audience.

Cosplay is a Japanese term coined by shortening two words: costume and play. Cosplay is a type of expression of pop culture from computer games and comics to board games and films or TV – basically anything that is considered geeky or nerdy or has a strong following of fans. Cosplay is usually something that is worn to comic book, film and TV conventions, where fans congregate to appreciate and express their devotion to particular characters in pop culture. Cosplay costumes are incredibly accurate and well researched and usually feature particular characters emulated down to the last detail. Cosplayers tend to create their own outfits, some planning a year or more in advance. This allows time for the incredibly detailed costumes to be made by hand, often by designing exclusive patterns and spending incredible amounts of money on refining the look.

Cosplay can be a fascinating realm to delve into and should definitely be witnessed in real life. There are comic and fan conventions all over the world and the events nearest to you can be found by searching online. Conventions are a chance to meet like-minded people who share the same interests. Many cosplayers are very talented designers, and by attending conventions you can share tips with each other to find out how outfits are put together or unique looks created. Swapping ideas can lead to new insights into how to create items integral to a Steampunk wardrobe and will give you a chance to discuss materials and techniques. If you're feeling brave, you could even create a cosplay outfit and wear it to a convention. This would make it easier to approach other cosplayers to chat about costuming. You may even get people asking you how you made your outfit, which will give you a chance to share your ideas and make new friends.

Cosplay doesn't have to be themed

around a particular character at all; it can just be a chance for you to create fantastical outfits that may be a bit too outlandish for outdoor wear. Creating costumes can be a wonderful way of learning and practising new skills, especially those that may be difficult to achieve in everyday crafting and making.

In cosplay circles, Steampunk seems to peak and trough depending on what is popular at the time. When a particularly Steampunk-inspired game such as Bioshock was released, comic conventions were awash with many takes on outfits from the game. As with anything, as interest peaks in a particular subject so the convention scene becomes saturated with inspired looks.

A current trend in cosplay seems to be taking traditional characters and 'Steampunking' them up, particularly feminine classic literary characters, such as Ariel from Hans Christian Andersen's *Little Mermaid*. Other female comic book characters such as Catwoman and Wonder Woman have also been given a Steampunk makeover. Even pop culture films such as *Ghostbusters* are not safe from the Steampunk treatment. It seems in Steampunk circles that the re-imagining of classic characters is a welcome and interesting task for many cosplayers and creates some interesting and definitive looks. Comic conventions sometimes go so far as to have a Steampunk day, where the style is encouraged and applauded by attendees. Convention goers create all manner of fantastical adventure-inspired outfits. The resulting congregation is one of the most photographed days at certain conventions, as people appreciate the hard work that goes into creating such highly detailed costumes.

There is a vast amount of information online about cosplay, including documentaries and whole websites dedicated to the craft, where you can see what others have made. The cosplay world is mainly online, apart from at conventions, so it is possible to carry out research without actually attending a convention. But to really appreciate the costumes first hand, it is best to try and go. Some conventions hold very useful costume creation workshops that are worth attending to pick up some hints and tips. Try looking at YouTube as there are many vloggers (video bloggers) who have whole channels dedicated to the genre and these are an invaluable source of inspiration and techniques. Through researching cosplay, you should be able to discover a new realm of untapped hints and tips that will help you build your Steampunk look and give it a polished finish.

It's Not All Cogs and Ray Guns

Individualism in Steampunk and how to incorporate your own style into your Steampunk look

When considering your foray into Steampunk, you need to include your own personal style. Quite often when I chat with my fellow creative friends, we claim to have one personal problem in common: a lack of style. This is, of course, just internalized cynicism on our part as in reality everyone has a style which can be distinguished, usually by a peer. After taking the time to discuss the ins and outs of unique personal style with friends, it turns out that you alone cannot discern your own personal sense of style. For example, a friend told me that I use a lot of opulent golds, burgundies and metallics in my work, which I had never noticed until it was pointed out to me. This also goes for fashion. I am a fan of the understated blazer, plain vest top, statement necklace, large rings and a skinny-legged jean or wet-look leggings which can be dressed up or dressed down as necessary. I had never realized how much I liked this look, though, until someone pointed out that whenever they see me at jewellery shows and fairs this is my usual dress code.

So chat with your friends or take a really close look at your closet to see what you really wear. I have a wardrobe overflowing with tons of garments but the old adage that people only wear ten per cent of their clothing is correct. I know I go back to the same items again and again because they are comfortable, fit for purpose or have something about them I click with. Humans are creatures of habit and we like routine, and it's no different when it comes to our wardrobe. There is, of course, nothing wrong with this as it displays our own sense of self to others along with our own sense of style. It may just be a particular colour that you are drawn to or it may be a particular type of top that you are fond of, but sometimes there are ways to break out of this box and to find yourself something new to incorporate into your day-to-day garments.

I like to add bits of Steampunk into my usual clothing style as that way I find it's not too overpowering. A full-on Steampunk look is great if you're going out or for a party of some sort, but not for everyday wear as it can be quite impractical. The thought of dragging a bustle onto the London Tube fills me with dread! On a personal level I like to add a nice updo with a pretty fascinator to the blazer and jeans combo. A nice brooch of some sort on the blazer adds in a few elements of Steampunk without turning the outfit into a costume, which is something you want to avoid in a daytime look.

There's nothing better than being confident and comfortable in what you're wearing and that will give you more of a sense of style than adding a

My usual day-to-day outfit.

certain item to an outfit. Steampunk has a synonymous relationship with cogs and ray guns and it's very easy to turn an item of clothing or jewellery into this style. However, I hope through making the projects in this book that you can step past the simple cog and ray gun and make something special for yourself. Your own personal style will then show through and your outfits will sparkle with Steampunk elegance!

Steampunk's obsession with creativity and how to DIY your own items through making the projects in the book

In Steampunk culture it is positively encouraged to be creative and to work on your own clothing and costumes. This comes from influences in the cosplay world where it is highly frowned upon if you refuse to make your own costumes for comic conventions and buy a ready-made piece. Whole conventions are dedicated to Steampunk all around the world, where like-minded people join together to show off certain Steampunk creations they have made with their own fair hands. These conventions are highly attended and feature classes for people to learn techniques from experts in the Steampunk field. Those who create items are also judged on their authenticity and craftsmanship.

Once you've tried a few projects in this book, have a go at seeing if you can upcycle your own items. It's amazing what you can do with an hour and a bag of scrap fabric. Your creativity will know no bounds once you get started. Try something basic for your first project and be prepared for it not to turn out as well as the picture you had in your head. This is nothing to be ashamed of – much practice and learning must happen before you master a technique. A failed project is never a wasted project, it's a learning curve.

Steampunk is a fairly DIY genre and making something yourself means that you will not only have a completely unique item, but a talking point too. Once you've unleashed your creativity by completing a few projects in this book, you should be able to start creating your own pieces.

Use the techniques described here and try to transpose them to your own work. Using resources like the chapter on mood boards will help you when designing new projects. Following the materials list will help you gather a core collection of items and tools, which means you can start projects easily with no real cost outlay for your basic resources. Be mindful of costs and research fully before you begin projects and you will find yourself creating plenty of things before too long.

Chapter 2
Materials and Equipment

Jewellery-making can become a minefield of miscommunication if you're not quite sure about the terminology you should be using. It is essential that you learn to tell your bead wire from your bell cap to avoid any mistakes in the creative process and with ordering supplies. Throughout this chapter you will learn the correct terminology for all things jewellery-related. These are the basic terms you will need to get you going on projects in the book. You can always pop back to this chapter at any time to refresh your memory should you need to.

Terminology

The main types of jewellery you will be making in the following tutorials are commonly metal-based, so it is best to learn what types of metal you would like to use. As these pieces are costume jewellery, stay away from precious metals and stick with something reasonably cheap and easy to use like mixed metals or plated metals such as gold and silver plate. Sterling silver is also a good choice when it comes to making items as it suits most people.

Metals can be tricky as they can cause allergic reactions. Chances are you will already know what metals you can wear. It's best to go with a plated metal for the main skin contact areas, so for things like chains, which will be worn directly on the skin for long periods, it should be something durable, ideally with a thicker plating. Have you ever bought a ring from a high street retailer that's given your finger a green tinge? Well, it's more than likely it was a mixed metal piece. The chances are the material that turned your finger green was a copper-based metal inside the mixed metal. Copper is not harmful to wear in direct contact with the skin, but once it has oxidized it will start to turn your skin green, which is not aesthetically pleasing and is often attributed to cheap jewellery.

Using plated metal is a great alternative to pure materials as it reduces your costs. However, plating will not last forever and will eventually wear away, exposing the mixed metal underneath, which will start to oxidize. To stave off the accelerative nature of oxidation, make sure you clean your jewellery regularly and try where possible to always wear it over the top of clothing so it has minimal contact with your skin's natural oils and sweat. Oil and sweat from skin will quickly deteriorate metals, so make sure you coat any close contact pieces with a suitable metal jewellery varnish. These varnishes are particularly useful for allergy sufferers as they can turn most metals into pieces that can be worn repeatedly. An added advantage is that you can top up the coating as and when it depletes, meaning that the metal itself should last a long time and show no signs of wear and tear.

Knowing what jewellery finding you require can be very difficult to discover if you're not *au fait* with the correct terminology. If you know the shape you need or if you can locate the piece already on another piece of jewellery, take it to your local haberdashery and they should be able to locate the right piece for you or at least be able to tell you what it's called. There is also a lot of information online, with detailed listings featuring all the jewellery findings you could possibly need. Some jewellery findings are very specific and will only be able to be used for certain tasks, so be aware of quantities when ordering online. As a general rule, the more quantity you buy of a finding, the cheaper it becomes. However, if you know that you only need a small quantity to complete one individual piece, it will be more cost-effective to just buy the amount you require than to have a surplus.

LEFT: Tools of the trade.

Tools

To get yourself started, you will need to put together a basic kit.

Simple tool kit:
1 pair of long-nosed pliers
1 pair of diagonal wire cutters
1 pair of round-nosed pliers
1 jump ring opening/closing band.

This simple kit will allow you to do a variety of things to begin with. Once you progress with your skills, you may need to change or add to it. You can quite often buy second-hand kits from eBay, but the tools themselves shouldn't be too expensive to buy new. Buy a decent-priced core kit as you will be using the tools a lot and you don't want them falling apart quickly. Also, think of comfort when you are buying; simple things like reinforced handles and padded grips will serve you well and make the creative experience more enjoyable. If you're left-handed, make sure the tools will work for you before buying. Some pliers have a grooved edge only on one side and you don't want to end up having to work backwards.

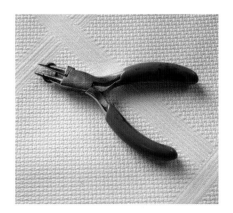

My trusty round-nosed pliers from my own jewellery-making kit.

Chains

Chains come in a variety of guises and it can be daunting to know what to buy. Very few jewellers make their own chains as it is costly and incredibly time-consuming. However, a good trick is to create the final chain by adding a clasp at the back and a large jump ring or connector to hold the chain together.

Tones of chain

It is worth buying different coloured chains as they can add to the overall aesthetic of the piece of jewellery you are making. As stated above, make sure you check your metals before purchasing an item.

The most common tones of chain tend to be gold and silver. These two colours come in a multitude of shades. A darker, antiqued gold rather than a bright gold tends to age better and looks worn-in, which easily ages an item (a good look in Steampunk circles). Bright gold is also beautiful and has a tendency to make an item look expensive without the additional cost.

Chains come in a variety of different link sizes and styles and you should pick the one that is most suitable for your project. Some links are easy to work with as they will hang down in a sequential pattern and make it easy to follow where your next jump ring needs to go. Others are twisted or sometimes cabled and can be very difficult to work with.

You will also need to be aware that different chain links will require different-sized jump rings. This is especially important when working with a very small-linked chain. Sometimes even the smallest jump rings won't fit through the tiny links. You should aim for a link size of 3 x 2mm and larger. This will fit most jump rings and make it easy to choose the correct size. When choosing a jump ring to fit the link of the chain, be certain to use the size nearest

An example of an antiqued gold-colour rolo chain.

to the size of the link. This will make the jump ring close to invisible and make it look like it's part of the chain itself. You can even use discarded links as jump rings, although sometimes the structural integrity of these on their own isn't as strong as that provided by the correct finding.

Some chains, such as box link, cable and snake chains, cannot have jump rings passed through them due to their solid structure, so you would need to place jump rings around the chain. This is not the best option as it can look unfinished and make the pendant slide around on the chain, which doesn't give such a professional look. However, it will work for some styles and shouldn't be ruled out completely.

You can buy plated chains in gold and silver and they are usually only slightly more expensive than standard mixed metal chains. Pick the tone you think will best suit your project and/or skin needs, then search retailers to find the best deal. Independent retailers usually tend to be cheaper and you can get great deals when you buy in bulk. However, for a small project, a local haberdashery can be a good source for pre-made plated chains.

Clasps for chains are very important and you should take into account how easy they are to open and close. A clasp should be secure and be able to hold the weight of the necklace. The usual rule to follow is that the bigger the necklace, the larger the clasp. Some smaller clasps are very strong and will hold a lot of weight, but this may make them difficult to remove afterwards.

A standard lobster clasp is suitable for most projects and they're available in a variety of colours to match most chains. There are other clasps such as spring rings, which can be very fiddly to operate but will work just as well. Hooks are an authentic choice for Steampunk as they're synonymous with Victorian jewellery; however, they can easily come undone if not paired with a spring-loaded clasp. Bar and toggle clasps work well for necklaces as they are kept closed by the weight of the piece, but they're not recommended for bracelets unless teamed with a safety chain as they can easily come undone. Once you have decided on a clasp that works for your designs, you will find it becomes an obvious choice for your projects.

A lobster clasp.

Basic Jewellery Findings

To start a small project, buy just a few jewellery findings from a haberdashery or craft shop. When purchasing jewellery findings, invest in a storage tray for different pieces. This will make it much easier when it comes to selecting the pieces you need and will keep them well organized. Most findings come inside small resealable bags, which makes them easy to locate when you need them. Depending on the way you like to organize yourself, you could empty the bags into a tray, use a pill organizer which makes great jewellery storage, or you could place the bags into one box using post-it notes to label each type of finding. Organizing your findings will save you time and also money in the long run as it is very easy to think you have run out of an item if it is not methodically ordered.

If you are thinking of creating more than just a few projects, it would be worth purchasing a jewellery-making kit to cut down costs. A kit will provide you with a good selection of findings that you can experiment with and use to grow your skill set.

A good kit should consist of the following items:
   Ear wires
   Jump rings in various sizes from 3mm
      to 7mm
   Lobster clasps in your preferred shade
   Beading wire
   Beading elastic
   Head pins
   Eye pins

Some other findings you may want to purchase when you have tried a few of the projects are:

   Ribbon crimp beads
   Pendant connectors
   Extender chains

A selection of jump rings.

Cabochon bails.

Larger and smaller jump rings,
   1.5mm–10mm
Cabochon bails
Brooch pins
Ring backs

Making a Standard Necklace Chain

First, gather all the items you need to make the chain:

Pair of round-nosed pliers and long-nosed pliers
Chain
Lobster clasp
2 large jump rings, 7mm or larger

Step 1: Measure your chain to the desired length. A standard-length necklace chain is eighteen inches long. This will reach to the base of your neck. If you have a wider than average neck, allow an extra inch to the length.

Step 2: Once you have your chain measured, take your pliers and separate the link after the eighteen-inch mark by sliding the link over the tip of your long-nosed pliers. Depending on the strength

of the chain, you can usually slide the link towards the thicker end of the plier and it should widen enough to unhook the attached link from it. If your chain is strong, use the tip of the pliers to force the link apart by opening the pliers.

Step 3: Once you have your length of chain, take your lobster clasp and clip it onto one of the jump rings. This ensures that your lobster clasp is working. Take the other jump ring and use your pliers

Measure the chain.

Separate the link from the rest of the chain.

Lobster clasp closed around the jump ring.

Open the jump ring to a 'C' shape using the pliers.

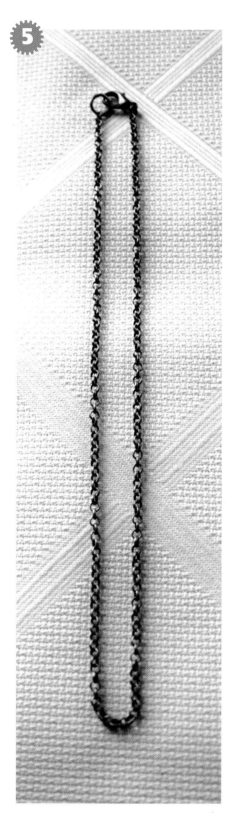

5

to open up the ring so it resembles a 'C' shape. Now use the end loop of the length of chain to hook onto the open jump ring. Use your round-nosed pliers to close the ring by squeezing gently but firmly on the edges of the open 'C'; it should begin to close. Don't squeeze too hard or else you will bend the jump ring out of shape.

Step 4: Take the other jump ring out of the lobster clasp and repeat the same

steps, turning the ring into a 'C' and hooking it through the opposite end of the length of chain. This time don't close the ring. Now take the lobster clasp and slide the circled end onto the open jump ring. Close the jump ring using the technique as before.

Open the lobster clasp and close as you would a normal necklace. And there you have it — your first chain!

Finished, standard-length, eighteen-inch rolo jewellery chain with lobster clasp closure.

Chapter 3
Design and Mood Boards

It is one thing to mortify curiosity, another to conquer it.
– ROBERT LOUIS STEVENSON

Design

As we all know, there are a few pieces of jewellery in our collections that we return to again and again. Ask yourself what it is about these pieces that you like so much. Is it their pure beauty? Is it because they are versatile and fit with almost all your outfits? Or is it because of their sentimental connection?

I own a simple black Victorian mourning ebony rosary that I bought from an antiques market and, even though I am not religious, its simplicity and large size make enough of a statement. The beads are somewhat worn, a few have had to be redrilled to stop them from disintegrating, the crucifix is tarnished gold and held on with a rather suspicious-looking sharp piece of wire, but there is beauty in revamping something that was clearly loved by its many previous owners.

My rosary has history, and the fact that it has been fixed several times and could, at any time, break and not be repaired adds a certain amount of romanticism to the piece. Who wore it? Who made it? What's its history? These are all questions that flutter through my mind when I wear my beloved rosary and they are also the questions asked by people when I tell them about my necklace. Part of the charm is not knowing the answers, a sense of mystery to behold. Regardless of its origins, my beloved rosary works with a multitude of outfits and this is the definition of great design.

The ability to create pieces that are timeless and can transcend trends is a great skill to have. Design and functionality are two things that go hand in hand and jewellery-making is no exception to this rule. It's all very well creating an item, but if it is not functional and fit for purpose then it becomes unwearable and it will soon find itself tucked in a drawer, never to be worn again.

The materials you choose in your design process need to be flexible, malleable and work with the body. Chain and fabrics work well as they are tried and tested. Always try to base your ideas on what you know. Fluidity and form are good principles of design when it comes to fashion. As you begin to create, you will find your curve and your style; if you discover a material that you like, experiment and see how it works. Always be careful of using materials that can damage skin or clothing.

FOLLOW THE RULES

If you make any jewellery to sell, make sure you're insured with public liability and product insurance to protect yourself legally and also your stock. Check the laws in the country you're selling your jewellery in and make sure you're abiding by all the trading laws for a small business. Following the rules from the inception of your business may be hard to begin with and seem unnecessary, but it will make things much easier in the long run.

Mood Boards

Design is complex and personal. When making a mood board, have an end goal in sight. This doesn't have to be the finished product, but you need a few ideas to make the process flow. For example, if you know you want to make a fascinator with a prominent use of leather and the colour gold, that's a good start. But if you want to make a small ring with a cog attached to it, then you probably don't need to go through

LEFT: My beloved antique Victorian ebony rosary necklace.

the mood board process.

Mood boards allow you to refine your working, assess your design process periodically and question your methods. Do you really need so many components to make that necklace? Or could you simply take the piece back to its bare bones? Of course the design process is the most important part of making an item, and using a mood board can save you hours of working on a project to later find it just doesn't work.

Before you start a project you need to map what you would like to make and how you would like to execute it. This should include important design DNA such as your original idea, cost of materials, cost to manufacture, cost to market the item and cost to distribute and to send to the shelf. You should also factor in other elements that may not seem important, such as how much time it will take to make, postage costs for materials and anything else that may be required such as specialist equipment hire, etc. If you're making an item for yourself, not all of these elements will apply, but it's always worth thinking through a project to avoid any hidden problems.

Once you're happy that you can afford to make the item, factoring in both cost and time, you're ready to go ahead. Should you find that an idea is too fanciful to make at this stage, don't throw it away, hold onto it. You never know when you may be able to think of an easier way to create it, or a technological advance will be invented and provide you with the equipment to create it.

Mood boards can contain a lot of different aspects: colours that inspire you, items of design. I see pieces of architecture or plants that may have a shape that will transpose perfectly to a motif. Create a mood board based on you and your inspirations. It can be a physical board or a document on a

Example of a dynamic photograph to use for a mood board by Charis Talbot Photography. The tones in the model's hair and also the background provided inspiration for an autumn/winter collection for Devine Delinquents.

computer, whatever you feel comfortable with. You can have an online board through a website like Pinterest or you can simply make a board in a Word or Powerpoint document.

Our influences and inspirations are what create our unique style and even though it's tempting to borrow heavily from one area or another, combining all your influences will create a strong sense of self in your work. Personally, when I'm designing, my ideas can come from anywhere but my main inspirations are mainly natural: rain, animals, rocks and crystals, herbs, stars and planets, feathers, contrasting textures like gravel and silk. I find looking at photographs and paintings evokes some great ideas for hues of colours. Religious paintings have some lovely tones and opulent colours that can be drawn upon and transposed into your own designs. These inspirations can sometimes be hard to detect in my work but that's because, through using mood boards, they become deeply combined with other influences of mine – like antique shops, car boot sales and flea markets, taxidermy, my love of gold and brass, antique lace, crochet and '90s pop culture.

All in all, you can draw your inspiration from anywhere. I continually add current inspirations to a mood board and revisit them a few months later. This leaves time for any faddy ideas to dissipate and the real ones to stick. This will give you a good constantly changing base from which to pick ideas and should mean that you never find yourself in a design slump.

Mood board exercise

Think of some things that you find inspirational and jot them down. Now find some pictures that you find inspirational and add them to your board. Feel free to add items like fabric you have found or any particular materials you think will work well with your project.

Include a sketch of your design as this will be your reference point for the whole mood board. It can be difficult to sum up your thoughts in the form of images so don't get too frustrated if you can't find the perfect images for your board. If it is only you working from and referencing your mood board, it only has to make sense to you. I often collaborate with people on a mood board for projects; it's a very useful tool to see how other people interpret an idea and means you can work together and bounce off each other.

When you have a basic board, think of your original idea and see if your board inspires you to make any changes. Once you are happy with your board, step away for a day or two and then go back to it. Quite often designers say looking at an idea with fresh eyes helps to spark new ideas or create clarity on an existing design. When you are happy with your board, begin to create your design.

You can also use mood boards when you are trying to think of new ideas. Sometimes I'll find myself with a colour stuck in my head for days and I will be able to pick it out in things I see during the days that follow. Quite often in my work my colour palette is fairly muted so I like to occasionally use a really bright colour to take me out of my comfort zone. Try using a material or colour that you wouldn't normally be drawn to and see how it affects your ideas.

Once you have a cohesive board, try creating a board that is completely different from any ideas you may have. For example, if you like dark colours, try using only bright elements. If you're usually drawn to light and diaphanous fabrics or materials, try heavy ones. You will be surprised at how quickly your brain will add its own unique spin on unfamiliar territory and start to adapt to working with interesting and new materials, enabling you to grow your design skill set.

Chapter 4
Necklaces

4

Gardens are not made by singing 'Oh, how beautiful,' and sitting in the shade.
– RUDYARD KIPLING

Most of the necklaces in this section start with the simple chain tutorial base. If you'll be doing a few tutorials in one day, make a few chains before you begin so you can spend time on the trickier parts of the tutorials. Necklaces can be worn as part of everyday outfits and being able to make your own is a valuable and money-saving skill. Any event you're planning to attend will provide a valuable opportunity to practise your skills and make something unique. Throughout the necklace tutorials, take time to repeat any steps you may find tricky as this will build your confidence and skill level, resulting in a more established proficiency in the craft of jewellery-making. Most importantly, have fun while making the projects and try not to impose time constraints on yourself as this added pressure can impede your rate of learning. Once you have mastered the simple techniques, transpose them into your own designs and create your own unique jewellery.

Tutorial 1: Simple Cog Necklace

For the first tutorial I have chosen a Steampunk staple, the humble cog. Steampunk is so much more than just cogs but, as a capsule piece and something that can add a tiny amount of futuristic engineering to an everyday outfit, you can't go wrong with a simple, effortless cog necklace.

Simple cog necklace.

LEFT: Linked cog necklace. (Photo by Twisted Pix)

31

For this tutorial you will need:
- 18in chain (see 'Making a standard necklace chain' in Chapter 2)
- Small cog
- 3–4mm jump ring

Tools:
- Round-nosed pliers
- Flat-nosed pliers

Step 1: Gather all your materials together.

Step 2: Take your pre-made chain and unclasp the lobster clasp. Lay the chain stretched out in one length on a flat surface. Find the centre of your chain by estimating where it would be with your finger. Pinch the chain between your thumb and forefinger and pick up off the flat surface. Hold the chain so both ends are hanging down and adjust your grip till both ends of the chain are hanging equally and touching each other. (Tip: allow for the length of the lobster clasp when doing this so you get a true centre point.) Once you have located the centre of your necklace, hold onto it with your other hand and if necessary mark with a piece of sticky tape.

Step 3: Take the 3–4mm jump ring and prise open with your pliers.

Step 4: Take the open jump ring and hang your cog on it and use the open jump ring to slot through the centre link of your chain. Tip: some jewellery makers close their jump rings around their chains instead of through the links so you end up with the pendant sliding around the chain. This is not an ideal way to finish your project as it will cause your chain to easily tangle in your clothing and the necklace will often end up slipping so that the clasp is at the front.

Step 5: Close the jump ring with your pliers and clasp your necklace back

Materials for the simple cog necklace.

Find the centre point of the chain.

Open the jump ring.

Hook the open jump ring through the cog and the chain.

Finished simple cog necklace.

together to complete the piece.

Tutorial 2: Cameo Necklace

Cameo necklaces are some of the most iconic pieces of jewellery from the Victorian period and a staple of the Steampunk genre. Traditional cameos were carved in a variety of colours and styles from shells or stones and could take months to complete. Due to their size and complexity, precision tools were and still are used to make the intricate shapes that form the image. The process

Cameo necklace.

easy to acquire and much cheaper than their traditional counterparts.

For this project I have chosen a resin cameo, as Steampunk mainly focuses on using costume jewellery instead of high-end, high-value pieces. You can purchase resin cameos at most haberdasher's or online. They come in a multitude of designs and colours and you should be able to find something to fit your project. Resin cameos are often referred to, particularly online, as 'cabochons'. This is an incorrect term as a cabochon actually refers to a polished stone of some sort, but it will be useful to use when trying to source your item.

You will also need a base to insert your cameo into, referred to as a base, frame or back. Cameo bases can be just as diverse as their centerpiece so, as a rule, try to make one of the two items more simplistic so that the two items complement each other.

As Steampunk has a link to all things Victorian and curio, I will be using a bat skull cameo for this necklace. I believe

of making a traditional cameo is lengthy, delicate and time-consuming.

There are two traditional methods of making a cameo. The first is carving into the base material and making a relief image, causing shadows to be projected on the item defining the details of the portrait or picture. The second method is to carve from the back of the material to produce a raised image on the front of the cameo.

Cameo production is still a popular pastime and can be a way of remembering a loved one or a certain occasion. However, due to the delicate process, carved cameos can be very costly. In the last few years, with the development of resin jewellery becoming popular, highly detailed cameos can now be made quickly and easily through using a simple mould and pour technique. This has made cameos

A selection of resin cameo designs.

A few types of cameo frames.

production, it is advisable to add texture to both surfaces to allow a better bond to form once the glue is applied to the components. However, be aware that the surfaces which are sanded will need to be hidden post-gluing so as not to look messy.

If you do make a mistake at this stage with sanding, depending on the size of the error, you may be able to sharpen the cameo or frame by applying a thin layer of PVA glue all over the piece to fill in any scrapes.

Step 5: Use a thin to medium layer of strong jewellery adhesive along the edges of the cameo and the base and press both pieces firmly together until they feel superficially bonded. Leave the cameo flat, facing upwards to dry. Depending on the adhesive you have used, the glue should be completely dry within twenty-four hours and ready for the next step.

Step 6: Take the bail and add a small dab of adhesive to the textured recess tray. Carefully attach to the back top centre of the cameo base so the loop is touching the frame, and leave to dry completely for twenty-four hours.

Step 7: Once the glue is completely dry on the bail, attach the cameo onto the chain. Take the centre point of the chain and use a sturdy and strong jump ring in a colour that matches or complements the frame, chain and bail. Open the jump ring and slide through the bail. Use the centre link on the chain to push the open jump ring through. Close with a pair of flat-nosed pliers or jump ring closer.

Now your cameo is finished, take care of it by storing it in a cloth bag when it's not being worn. These can be purchased at most craft shops or you could make your own in a fabric you find appealing. You can do this by simply cutting a

this gives an edgy style – something I aim for within my designs. Should you wish to soften your design, you could use a portrait or floral piece. You could also think about adding some extras to your design, such as hanging beads or feathers, which will add to the overall feel and aesthetic.

For this tutorial you will need:
  18in length of chain in a colour of your choice
  Lobster clasp
  2 x 4mm jump rings
  Cameo setting in a colour of your choice
  Large glue-on bail
  Cameo of your choice

Tools:
  Round-nosed and flat-nosed pliers
  Strong jewellery glue
  Small piece of sandpaper or emery board

Step 1: Gather all materials together before you begin. This is particularly important as you will be using quick-drying glue.

Step 2: Make a standard eighteen-inch necklace chain, locate the centre point and set aside for later.

Step 3: Take your cameo and cameo base and place the cameo onto the base to test that the cameo fits correctly and that the back is level and sound. Make sure the base is the right way up, with any frame details pointing in the right direction. It is best to rectify any potential mistakes at this stage before gluing as it will be very difficult or impossible to do so afterwards.

Step 4: Take the cameo out of the frame and use the sandpaper or emery board to very carefully roughen the edges that will stick to the base. As some cameos and bases can be too smooth after

Gather your materials together.

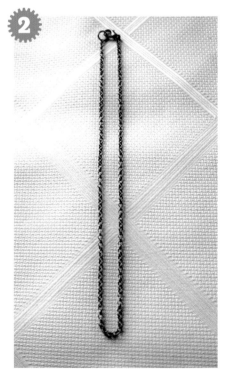

Standard length necklace chain.

Check the cameo fits correctly in the frame.

Sand the edges of the cameo if needed.

Add a thin layer of glue to the cameo edge and base.

Attach the bail to the top of the frame.

Attach the bail to the chain.

The finished cameo necklace.

square of fabric and using a strong fabric glue to bond the edges together. Do this inside out and then turn the square the right side out to finish and add a square of velcro to the inside top edge to hold firmly closed and keep the cameo safely inside the bag.

Tutorial 3: Ray Gun Necklace

Ray guns are synonymous with all things Steampunk and are an easy way to add a distinct and definite air of the genre to any outfit. There are no hard and fast rules as to what they have to look like. You can be as daring or as understated as you wish. Ray guns are the embodiment of kitsch within this style and allow you to experiment with your design process.

To begin with, you may wish to look at actual weaponry to gain a clear idea of what you are aiming for. Start with a simple sketch of the standard sideways 'L' of a gun and then build around this shape.

1950s B movie weapons are a great source of inspiration and will provide some great shapes to consider. A lot of these '50s movies have bright, shiny, post-war, utopian ray guns, whereas your necklace should be a little more distressed and look as if it's been through an apocalypse or left out in the rain for months. Consider the backstory of your 'gun'. What was it used for? Where has it been? Did you find it or did you make it yourself? All of these things will make your item truly personal and unique.

For this tutorial you will need:
  18in length of chain in a colour of
    your choice
  Lobster clasp
  3 x 4mm jump rings
  Small water pistol
  Large glue-on bail
  2 tablespoons of acrylic paint in a

metallic shade of your choice
3 or 4 small cogs or other small watch mechanics

Tools:
  Round- and flat-nosed pliers
  Strong jewellery glue
  Paintbrush
  Toothpick

Ray gun necklace.

Step 1: Gather all your materials together before you begin and pick out the cogs or small mechanics you would like to use on your necklace. Place the mechanics on the parts of the gun you would like to decorate and make a quick sketch of where they sit best or take a photograph to capture their placement. Once you have made a note of the placement, remove the adornments and move to the next step.

Step 2: Take the paints you have chosen and pour a small amount, around one and a half tablespoons, of the main colour for your necklace into a disposable plastic cup or similar. Using acrylic paint is best as it will stick to the plastic of the gun underneath and provide a good medium-wearing coverage. If you want the paint to be very long-wearing, use a small amount, around one teaspoon, of craft glue mixed with the colour; this will allow the paint to adhere strongly to the plastic and provide incredibly long-lasting coverage. Mix the paint thoroughly before use to allow for even coverage. Apply a thin layer of paint all over the gun, paying special attention to the underside and easily neglected crevices and nooks. Once you've applied a full thin layer, leave to dry upon a sheet of cling film (shrink wrap) for one to two hours until touch dry. Repeat the last step until the gun is thoroughly covered and the original paint colour is disguised or muted.

Step 3: Once your gun is touch dry, pour out around half a tablespoon of the second colour for your gun. Depending on the style you would like to create, you can use this colour to neatly pick up the raised areas of your gun or to add a messy rusted look. To apply the neat look, you will need to slowly apply the paint carefully and delicately, using a small brush and taking care to stick within the

Begin by gathering your materials together.

Choose the cogs you would like to use on your necklace.

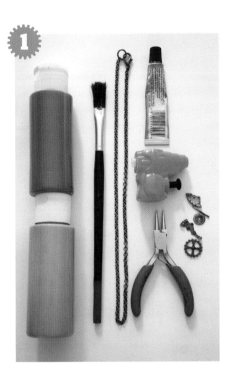

Paint the gun with the base colour.

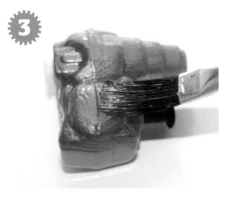

Use your second colour to add depth and dimension.

Glue all the mechanical decorations into place.

lines. If you would like to create a more post-apocalyptic style, you can use the paint to add texture and rust by adding splodges of paint onto the gun in areas which you think would naturally rust if it was made of metal. Once you have added your preferred style of painting, leave to dry overnight or for twenty-four hours until completely dry.

Step 4: Refer back to your sketch or photograph of the placement of your small mechanics and place upon the gun in your preferred areas. Take a toothpick and a strong jewellery adhesive and apply an adequate amount of glue to cover the back of the first cog. Use the dry end of the toothpick to manoeuvre the first piece into place and press down so the glue starts to bond with the plastic. Leave each piece to dry for around ten minutes before applying the next piece to avoid any accidental slippage. Once all the pieces are in place, leave to dry for twenty-four hours until completely dry.

Step 5: Take your finished gun and work out the centre point of each end. These are usually the areas that are the intake water area and the hole where the water is expelled. Remove any plugs or stoppers from the water chamber and dispose of them. Locate the centre point where the water is squirted from and use the tip of a small pair of round-nosed pliers to very gently depress the opening. Once you have managed to make a wider cavity within the water chamber, keep using the pliers to forge a wider opening until it is large enough to pass a length of chain through. Use a piece of cotton to test whether the water chamber and the water spray end can be joined in one continuous length of chain. If the cotton passes easily through the gun then you can proceed to the next step. However, if the cotton struggles to make a clean pass through the gun, you may need to widen the hole further or remove

some of the internal workings of the gun, such as the plastic tube which is used to carry the water to the tip of the gun. The plastic tube can be cut through with a small, sharp pair of scissors and the resulting waste can be removed with pliers. Once this is achieved, try passing the piece of cotton through again until it passes easily through the gun.

Step 6: Measure where you would like your necklace to sit by holding it on the preferred area of your torso. Take a length of chain and measure one length from the back of your neck to the preferred spot. Double the chain to make the full circumference of your necklace and thread through the hole in the gun. Once the chain is threaded through and the gun is central on the chain, attach a lobster clap and jump ring to finish the piece.

Now you have your ray gun necklace, use it to spice up a range of outfits, or style it with items you wouldn't usually think were Steampunk to create edginess. You will be surprised at the versatility of this stand-alone piece and how quickly you will want to make another in a different style. Experiment with colours and textures and different adornments when making it but remember to only add adornments to one side of your gun to avoid it getting tangled in clothing.

Use adornments you wouldn't usually think to use, such as glitter or small beads, as these will add texture but will not over-decorate your piece. If adding the small pieces becomes too fiddly and time-consuming, use metallic markers to draw filigree or mechanics directly onto the gun. This will also give flexibility in where to add decorative flourishes as you won't be bound by the ridges and raised areas on the gun, which are unable to hold attached embellishments due to their angled surfaces and inability to create a strong bond.

Use round-nosed pliers to create an entry point for the chain.

Guide the chain through the gun.

Finished ray gun necklace.

Tutorial 4: Leather Flower Necklace

Leather is a pliable and interesting material to work with. It's great for making shapes as it is durable yet flexible. Leather is a natural material so it weathers well and can be used for a multitude of projects. If this is your first time using leather, stick to a simple design and test your pattern on a scrap of fabric before committing to your final design. Sourcing leather can be costly but scraps can be picked up from most fabric shops, or if you plan to make a few pieces with leather you may want to order a sheet. Even old shoes, coats and bags can provide a valuable source of fabric, but beware when cutting as some deconstructed items might not provide enough material to finish the project. It's best to measure the size you need once you have drafted the shape you would like to use.

If you are opposed to using leather, there are plenty of decent animal-free replicas that can be picked up at most fabric shops or online. These leather substitutes are not as thick as normal leather so you will only need a standard fabric needle to sew them together; you could even glue them as they will hold easily with fabric glue.

For this project I have decided to make a flower shape, but you can make any shape you like. Once you've tried a basic shape, why not try something more complex like a cog or dragonfly to help build your skills?

For this tutorial you will need:
* 2–3 leather scraps in varying colours of your choice
* Leather glue or strong craft glue
* Sharp scissors or small rotary wheel fabric cutter
* Button or other suitable centre for your flower
* Standard 18in pre-made chain
* 1–2 eyelets in a colour to match or complement the chain
* 2 x 4 or 5mm jump rings in a colour to match the chain

Step 1: Before you start the practical making of your necklace, you will first need to sketch a final design of what you would like your finished flower to look like. The shape you design for your individual petals will form the blueprint of your design. Consider when sketching that your flower should sit flat against your skin, so the piece will require a level base section.

Step 2: Once you have a sketched design, deconstruct the individual shapes of your flower and sketch them onto the reverse of the pieces of leather you have chosen. A biro or pencil will mark the leather easily and will give you a discernable line drawing to follow. Should you make a mistake while drawing on the reverse of the leather, sketch the line again and put an 'X' through the mark you don't wish to be part of the design. This will alert you when it comes to the cutting stage and you should then avoid any further mistakes and waste of materials. Using

Leather flower necklace.

Gather your materials together.

Sketch your design before you begin to define the shape of your flower.

two different tones of leather for your petals will create depth and make your design look more accomplished. Layering of the two colours in a staggered pattern can create a pleasant effect. Once you have cut your petals, you can arrange them before committing to a final construction and gluing the pieces in place.

Step 3: Take a pair of sharp scissors or a small rotary cutter and cut the first set of petals. Depending on the size you would like your flower to be and how much time you have, you can cut one circular base piece and attach individual petals to it in turn, or you can cut a base piece which contains petals. Turn your leather over and very carefully begin to cut with your scissors or roll your rotary blade over the lines. Remember to only ever cut once to avoid your leather having ragged edges. Once you have accumulated a pile of around twenty to thirty petals, you can begin layering them.

Step 4: Laying your base piece flat, take the leather glue and add a small dab to the edge of the petals you wish to stick down. To avoid getting your leather dirty, use a small paintbrush to add the glue or a bottle with a tapered applicator. Should you spill any glue on the front of your petals, you will need to discard the soiled piece and cut another as leather glue, once applied, cannot be removed easily or at all. Systematically layer the petals and repeat the gluing process until you have used them all.

Step 5: Once you have used all your petals and glued them into place, take the centre button or other charm you have chosen and add a dab of glue to the back. Make sure the top set of petals is as flat as can be and press the button down firmly. To avoid any spillage of glue from underneath the button, use a

sparing amount and layer if the first dab is not enough.

Step 6: Once glued down, the flower should be left overnight to dry

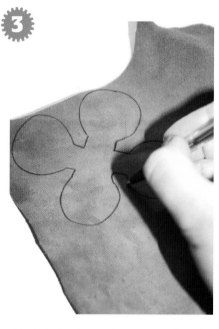

Mark the leather on the reverse side with the design.

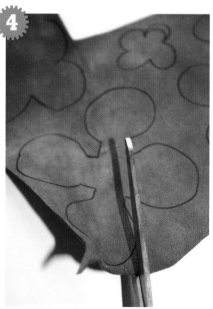

Cut out your petals.

completely. Place it on a clean protected surface and away from any possible disturbance. Once completely dry, take the flower and find the centre point of the top petal. Depending on the size of

Layer the petals and glue in place until they begin to form the final flower shape.

Glue the centre button into place.

the flower, you may wish to hang it by its centre so it has a pendulous look. If your flower is a larger design, it would be best suited to hang from two axis points, providing the piece with a strength in its core and avoiding any of the petals curling over time. Once you have found the point to hang your chain through, take the leather punch and gently pinch the leather without the eyelet loaded, to make a circular marking point. When you're happy with the location, load the eyelet into the leather punch and squeeze with a firm grip to push the eyelet through. The eyelet will flare to cover the hole and will protect it from fraying or tearing in the future. Eyelets make any leather work look professional and accomplished and will protect your piece over time.

Step 7: To finish your piece, very quickly pass a lighter over the edges of your petals to seal them and prevent any leather residue falling onto your clothing. Be aware that the flame could cause damage to the surrounding leather of your necklace, so use the lighter to sparingly lick the edges and repeat if the edges don't look completely sealed. The edges should develop a slightly darker tone to them and feel stiffer when sealed correctly. This step is only necessary for real leather as substitutes will most likely be flammable. Once you've completed sealing the edges, use a jump ring to slot through the eyelet, attach your chain and close using pliers.

Use the eyelet tool to insert an eyelet into the leather.

Finish the necklace by attaching the flower to the chain.

Tutorial 5: Cog Locket

A locket is a symbol of sentimentality and links nicely to Steampunk through its Victorian roots. Lockets were originally used to remember loved ones or to contain something as personal as a lock of hair or sometimes even teeth. Before photography had become widely available, early lockets had miniature portraits painted inside them. These paintings were often of the owner's family or significant other and were incredibly expensive to own due to the custom nature of the item and the skill required by the artist painting them. Lockets have remained a popular item within fashion throughout the ages, possibly because of their ability to be customized, meaning each piece is unique and personal to the wearer.

In the lockets I have made I have included personal keepsakes such as sand from a special holiday, leaves from a favourite walk and dried flowers from wedding bouquets. You could even scent a locket with a few drops of perfume or essential oils on tissue paper to remind you of a place or time. The more personalized you can make the locket, the more it will mean to you and help to evoke special memories when worn.

For this tutorial you will need:
Locket of your choice with a blank front to decorate
6–10 cogs and watch parts in various sizes
Standard 18in pre-made necklace chain
4–5mm jump ring

Tools:
Toothpick
Pair of round-nosed pliers
Pair of flat-nosed pliers
Pair of cat claw clippers
Strong jewellery adhesive

Step 1: To begin, gather all your materials and prepare your work space. As this is a tutorial using fast-drying glue, you will need to be ready to work quickly. First, take your locket and make sure the area where you will be attaching the cogs and watch parts is clean and dry. Use a dry cloth to dust the locket and prepare the area to be glued.

Take your selection of cogs and watch parts and arrange on the top of your locket to see where the pieces best fit.

The cog locket necklace.

This may take some patience and a few tries before you are satisfied with the arrangement. To allow items to be moved around more easily you can use a pair of thin-tipped tweezers – this will prevent you knocking your design around with your fingers every time you wish to move a piece around. Try layering cogs on top of each other or straying outside the constraints of the centre oval by using pieces that jut out over the edge. This will emphasize the Steampunk element and capture a wild, mad professor style to the piece. Should you wish to keep the item restrained and in more of a Victorian style, stick to staying inside the centre oval and use repeating patterns or symmetry.

Be aware of the front and also the back of your chosen pieces – they will need to be flat-backed or have a flat piece of surface area in order to adhere to the base or other parts successfully. Again, run a piece of sandpaper over the back of the trimmings if they're too smooth to stick solidly to the base. Once you have settled on a design for the embellishments, take a photograph or make a quick sketch. This will make it easier when it comes to gluing the pieces down, as you will have an easy reference to work from rather than relying on your memory.

Step 2: Remove all the cogs and adornments from the front of your locket and arrange them in the order you will need to glue them down. If you're layering the piece, you will need to work with the lower layers first, working up to the top layer. Set your photograph in front of your workspace so you have your reference to hand. If using a smartphone, tablet or laptop to display the reference photograph, make sure the automatic screen lock is turned off. This will avoid having to touch your chosen technology with potentially glue-covered fingers and will save you time in the long run.

Take the lowest layer of the watch parts and use a toothpick to add a few small dabs of strong jewellery adhesive to the back of the item. Once glued, slowly and carefully lower the item into its position, taking time to press down with the dry end of the toothpick on the glued areas. Make sure you firmly press the pieces down with an even force so as not to dislodge the part and spread glue across the front of the locket. Once in place, repeat the step several times, layering as you go and being careful and gentle to avoid moving the already placed items on the locket.

Step 3: Once you have most of the adornments in place, after an hour very carefully check the items have adhered by using your toothpick to tap the pieces gently. If the items stay firmly in their position, they will have adhered correctly. Should any of the items move, remove the piece from the locket and add a touch more glue before attempting to reattach.

Step 4: Once all your items have correctly adhered to the front of the locket, leave to dry for at least twenty-four hours before wearing. Thread the pre-made chain through the bail at the top of the locket, and attach with the jump ring by passing through the centre link and hanging the locket on it. Close the jump ring to complete the locket.

USING GLUE

The first dab of glue from a glue tube is best avoided as it will have already had some contact with the air and will have lost some of its chemical bonding elements. Dab the first half inch of glue onto some tissue and dispose of it before use to make sure you're getting the glue at its most adhesive.

Once you have completed your locket necklace, you can place anything inside it that you wish to keep near to you. On the internet there are many websites that will print locket-sized photos which can be sent to your door, even with an old-time sepia hue over your image for the complete Steampunk look. Why not set up a photoshoot at home of your loved one or even your pet with a Steampunk

Gather all the materials together before you begin, as you will require pieces to be available due to the quick-setting nature of the glue.

Prepare the cogs and mechanics ready to be glued into place.

Start gluing the adornments into place.

Remove and add more glue to any pieces that may not have adhered correctly.

Add the finished locket to the chain.

twist specifically for the interior of your locket? It will provide you with a wonderful memory everytime you open it as well as a great talking point.

Tutorial 6: Linked Cog Necklace

A large statement necklace is a great way of making an otherwise ordinary outfit extraordinary. The large linked cog necklace is a statement piece and can be used as a focal point for an everyday outfit. It nods to Steampunk without being overly extravagant, which allows it to be versatile and easily mixed with other accessories or fashion trends. The linked cog necklace is made up of several varying sizes of cog evoking ideas of machinery, but if you're not too keen on making something entirely with cogs, you could use some other charms to intersperse and break up the pattern.

When designing your piece, be mindful of creating something delicate to offset the size of the necklace. Statement necklaces sometimes have a tendency to look too bulky and lack the delicacy required to balance visual spectacle and wearable jewellery. Striking this balance can be a difficult thing to achieve when making something on a larger scale, as it's very easy to add unnecessary elements just to bulk the piece out. To make something simple, use the trick of adding in all the elements you would like to use and then removing two component parts. This will instantly make your design simple and elegant.

When designing this piece it is important to take your time and concentrate on the overall shape you would like to achieve. Take several different-sized cogs and place them together on your workspace and move them around until you get your desired shape. Switch some pieces in and out, try different colours together, stack cogs

on top of each other – the possibilities are endless and should be explored thoroughly before committing to your final motif. Once you're happy with the shape you have created, make a quick sketch of where the pieces are positioned or take a photograph. This will give you a basis from which to work and prevent any accidental knocks ruining your design.

For this tutorial you will need:
   10–20 medium-sized cogs, watch parts and other discarded mechanical pieces
   Approximately 20 x 5mm jump rings in a colour to match your cogs
   Approximately 20 x 7mm jump rings in a colour to match your cogs
   16in pre-made necklace chain

Tools:
   Round-nosed pliers
   Flat-nosed pliers

Step 1: Take the pre-made, shorter sixteen-inch necklace chain and split it into two at its centre link. The chain is made shorter for this design as the centre of the creation will create some of the girth of the necklace. Using a standard length chain would make the necklace too long and would result in the centre becoming distorted as it would not remain taught. Once the chain is split into two, add an open 7mm jump ring to either end. Leave the ends open as they will provide the hanging points for your centre design.

Step 2: Arrange the charms in the shape you would like your necklace to be and try a few variations of placement. A 'V' formation is a good template to work on or a wider 'U' shape, as these will enhance the shape of your neck and provide a complimentary structure to work from. Pay special attention to the holes that will connect your cogs together, as these will need to be facing in the correct direction. Once you have the shape of your design, take a photo for reference in case you knock any of the pieces out of the way by mistake.

Step 3: Begin to join your pieces together. Some elements will have suitably sized holes which will accommodate a jump ring easily. Other pieces will require smaller, thinner jump rings to fit through the openings. Start joining your pieces together from the centre and work outwards as this will allow you to build and add in extra cogs and mechanical elements if the piece isn't looking bulky enough. To make the process quicker, open the jump rings before you begin.

Step 4: Build the design outwards cog by cog on either side of the design so it grows evenly. Ensure your jump rings are closed at each connection securely by pressing together with flat-nosed pliers or a surprise tool in your arsenal – cat claw clippers, which are brilliant for closing jump rings. Claw clippers are incredibly strong and can be capable of causing injury so be careful if you do choose to use this tool. They will save you a lot of time in the long run as they are more precise than flat-nosed pliers and will require less adjustment of the rings while closing.

Step 5: Once you have finished building your large centrepiece, attach it to either end of your chain using the open jump rings from the first step. Finish by closing the jump rings and trying on the necklace. If the shorter length chain proves to be too short and is uncomfortable to wear, you can extend the chain either side by extending the chain inch by inch with a spare piece. Keep both sides equal when extending to avoid the necklace becoming lopsided.

Linked cog necklace.

1

For this tutorial, gather your materials before you begin and ensure you have enough cogs to complete the necklace.

Once your necklace is finished, try styling it with plain garments of clothing to make it stand out. Avoid wearing the piece over fabrics that will snag easily, such as silks and lace, due to the rough texture of some of the cogs.

2

Split the chain at its centre point and add a jump ring to either end.

4

Lay out the cogs in the shape you would like the necklace to be.

6

Close the rings, attaching the centre piece to the chain, and adjust if needed.

3

Begin to join the cogs together.

5

Begin to build upon the cogs until you have your desired shape.

7

Finished cog necklace.

Tutorial 7: Chain and Jewel Drop Necklace

Before you begin this tutorial, you need to focus on the design element and use the mood board method to create a template of your final piece. When coming up with the original idea for your necklace, think of Regency-inspired jewels, tiered necklaces and more elaborate black tie event jewellery. These types of jewellery, when worn historically, usually conveyed a message of wealth and high social standing in the Victorian era, as they often contained stones and precious metals which were difficult to acquire and therefore expensive. Your piece should refer to your own personal sense of style but will need to be even more elaborate in nature than you would usually wear: think opulence and wealth.

You will need several different components to make this necklace and you will have to try out different chains and jewels until you arrive at a combination you feel works for you. Try using a mood board to arrive at an amalgamation of elements that suits your style best and try using combinations that may not necessarily seem like obvious choices.

The chain and jewel drop necklace is a piece that can be used to accent a more elaborate outfit, and this is something to consider as you create your sketches for the final design. The design element of this piece will take longer than putting the piece together; again, use the 'less is more' approach when designing to make a stunning item.

For this tutorial you will need:
  Pre-made standard length necklace
    chain
  Extra length of chain to add
    decoration – around 1.5m should be
    sufficient
  3 jewels of your choice
  Handful of 3–4mm jump rings

Tools:
  Round-nosed pliers
  Flat-nosed pliers
  Jewellery bust

Step 1: Find the centre link of your pre-made chain and add the first gem using a jump ring. Close the jump ring holding the gem and place the necklace on a jewellery bust. If you don't have access to a jewellery bust, you can use a

Chain and jewel drop necklace.

coat hanger and hold the chain in place with a few strips of sticky tape. Using a jewellery bust makes it easier to work on the necklace as you won't need to keep moving the necklace around while creating it.

Step 2: To start creating the shape of your necklace, you need to begin working around the framework of the centre chain. Bear in mind the shape of your neck and how you would like the piece to sit around the decolletage. Creating tiered chains makes a delicate base and will frame the gems you have chosen, setting them off nicely. Try holding the chain up to your necklace and trying a few different variations; take photos of your favourites and refer back to what did and didn't work. Once you have decided on a style you would like, measure the pieces of chain and break the chains at the point necessary using round-nosed pliers.

Step 3: Hang the chains using the smallest jump rings possible so as not to draw attention to the joins. You could even use other links of the original chain to make the joins imperceptible. Once you have added the first few chains, you can then begin to see where the next points should be to hang the next two gems. Measure your necklace around a third of the way around from the clasp. This will give you the second point to hang your next gem. Attach with a jump ring and check that the gem hangs downwards instead of backwards. At this point, you may wish to try on the necklace to make sure it sits correctly across the clavicle and the gem doesn't point upwards or backwards. Repeat the same step on the opposite side of the necklace, checking that the gems are level.

Step 4: Mirror the chain around the other two gems and secure with chain

TRACE CHAINS

A trace chain is a large link piece of chain, usually around two inches in length, finished with a small charm. They are used to extend necklaces so they can fit a variety of neck sizes.

links or small jump rings using flat-nosed pliers. Be careful not to crush the chain links by gently closing them together. Should you make a mistake and accidentally crush a jump ring or link, remove it using your round-nosed pliers and try again. Once you have added all the extra chains, try on the necklace to make sure everything sits correctly and that the chains are connected to the right points and hang below the frame, not above. If things don't look quite correct, adjust and change the links until they sit more flush with the skin.

Begin to break the chains once you have measured them correctly on the base framework.

Attach the centre jewel collection to the middle of the chain.

Measure and begin to place the next gems on the chain.

4

Check that the necklace sits correctly by trying on or placing on the jewellery bust.

Step 5: To finish, check the jump rings to make sure they're closed securely and that the necklace fits correctly. If it doesn't, add a trace chain to extend the piece. The trace chain can also be used for added security by attaching a second link of chain onto the lobster clasp. This will stop the necklace from easily coming undone, especially if it's heavy.

5

5. Check the jump rings are securely closed.

Chapter 5
Brooches, Rings and Pins

To put up with what you cannot avoid is a philosophical principle, that may not perhaps lead you to the accomplishment of great deeds, but is assuredly eminently practical.
- JULES VERNE

Brooches are an easy way to add instant glamour to an accessory or outer garment. Decorative yet functional, brooches are a pretty way of fastening a scarf or blouse and can quickly become a staple in your jewellery collection. With a variety of styles and through experimentation, you can easily make something that becomes timeless and an everyday wearable piece. All brooches have a few elements in common and these can be combined in many ways to make something bold and beautiful or small and understated. It only takes a small amount of research to explore how many different styles have been adopted through the eras. Because of their practicality, brooches were used as early as the Bronze Age and have been found in a multitude of archeological digs. This is a testament to their versatility. They are pieces worth adding to your jewellery collection.

Rings are often used as a symbol of longevity and eternity, possibly because of their circular, unbreakable shape. Rings can be a quick jewellery piece to complete, with some projects taking less than thirty minutes. It is important to be practical with anything you wear on your hands as a ring needs to be able to withstand the daily tasks your hands undertake. If your ring is purely decorative and grandiose, I would recommend that you restrict it to costume wear only to preserve it for future use. The type of adhesive you use for rings is very important – it needs to be strong and durable to avoid breakages.

Pins can be attached to all manner of things, from hair to hats and scarves. The pins we will be focusing on will be safe, capped or covered pins. Uncovered pins are a traditional design feature and are historically authentic, but they can be sharp and dangerous. As you will be wearing your creations in everyday situations, it is important that they are practical and don't potentially cause you, or others, an injury. If you do decide to use uncapped or uncovered pins, be careful and mindful of this and place them in a prominent area, preferably with plenty of material behind them to prevent any accidents. Pins are not as common in modern everyday wear as they used to be in Victorian times, but that's what makes them an important addition to any outfit as they will create Steampunk authenticity.

Glues

Jewellery glue

Jewellery glue can be a tricky medium to work with for a variety of reasons, and it can be difficult to discover a glue that works perfectly first time. Techniques for brooches, rings and pins are fairly simplistic and very easy to execute once you have learned the basics of what will and won't work as far as adhesives are concerned. Certain types of glues are not suitable for jewellery-making as they will react with metals and cause them to corrode. When looking for adhesives for jewellery, always make sure that metal is listed on the packet as a suitable surface to bond with. Some glues will say that they will bond with metal but won't provide the long-lasting bond that you need from your jewellery to go through the knocks and scuffs of everyday life. It is also important to check that the type of metal you're using is safe to use with the type of glue you have chosen. Some

LEFT: Stick and go eyeball ring.

base metals which contain copper or other reactive materials could cause the piece to not adhere securely or to become discoloured.

A lot of jewellery and metal adhesives require care when using as they are very good at sticking anything and everything together. Some glues will have recommended methods of using them printed on the packaging, but it is advised that you try them on projects that aren't too precious to begin with, as it is likely that you will make mistakes in the initial testing stages of a product. Different glues will require different drying times and this should be considered when planning a timescale for creating a project. Most glues will have a recommended drying time printed on their packaging, but it is best to always overestimate drying times, rather than underestimate them, to allow for a secure bond. Some jewellery glues will be made using chemicals that can be harmful to the skin and require respirators to avoid inhalation. Do check manufacturers' instructions for recommended safety precautions before using a new product.

Fabric glue

There is a huge range of fabric glues on the market, each of which is suitable for different projects depending on the result you are trying to achieve. For most projects a standard all-round fabric glue will be fine. Sometimes, fabric glues are perfect for certain techniques, such as adding embellishments to fabrics. A tacking or hemming glue is a good choice for quick projects where only a small amount of fabric requires gluing. You should always try and sew fabrics if possible, but sometimes a project will be quick and not require a serious amount of stitching. This is where glue is perfect, as it is quick to use. Some glues, however, will require a long time to dry

and this can take longer than hand-stitching an area.

Fabric glues are best suited for layering fabrics or adding touches such as bows or flowers. It is not advisable to use fabric glues on areas that will be main seams on clothing garments as the adhesive can deteriorate over time and weaken or split. However, a glued accessory such as a hat, jabot or gloves may well hold up over time. When purchasing a fabric glue, try where possible to speak to a haberdasher first to get their recommendation on the most suitable type of adhesive for your project. If you're unable to visit a haberdasher in person, there are many places to research fabric glue on the internet.

Hot glue

For items like headbands, fascinators and hair combs, I would suggest using a hot glue gun. A glue gun is an easy way of producing a quick-drying, sturdy adhesive for larger scale projects. The glue gun works by heating a solid stick of glue through a heating element, which is then deployed by using a trigger to administer a small amount of very hot glue to a targeted area. Glue gun adhesive dries very quickly so is best used in small amounts during a project rather than covering a large area and sticking items down, as the glue will invariably have dried by then.

Hot glue is not ideal for joining metals together or for any projects where the hot glue would melt the material you are using. Hot glue will attach metal to fabric, but be careful as the metal will act as a heat conductor when you apply the glue and can cause burns. You can pick up a glue gun for a small amount of money from most craft shops. It is important to spend more on tools that you will use repeatedly: cheaper glue guns can break quickly and cause burns

from the melted adhesive, so it's best to invest in a decent branded version as it will last you a long time.

Tutorial 1: Simple Stick and Go Ring

A stick and go ring is a very quick, very easy tutorial to complete and is a simple way to make a great statement piece in a small amount of time. To begin, make sure you have all your materials together before you start as we are working with an adhesive so you will need to move quickly to avoid mistakes.

Stick and go rings make great gifts and can easily be personalized to make something special for a loved one or friend.

For this tutorial you will need:
Adjustable ring base in a colour of your choice
Cabochon or cameo in a matching size to the ring base or larger

Tools:
Strong jewellery adhesive
Flat-nosed pliers
Toothpick
Plasticine
Sandpaper or emery board

Step 1: Choose an adjustable ring base in a colour of your choice; these can be found at most haberdasher's for a small cost. Try the ring on and adjust till it fits the finger you would like to wear it on. To adjust the ring, slowly and gently pull either side open. Allow an extra millimetre for your finger to naturally swell so the ring doesn't get stuck. Avoid adjusting the ring when it is on your finger as you can pinch your skin between the gap in the metal.

Step 2: Check the adhesive base area of the ring and use a small piece of sandpaper or an emery board to add texture and provide a good surface for

Cameo stick and go ring.

surface. Push the base of the ring downwards so the top is facing upwards. Once the ring is stable and can stand upwards on its own you can begin to move the cameo or cabochon into place. Using the pliers, slowly lower it onto the ring base. Use the dry end of the toothpick to tap down on the surface to make sure the cabochon or cameo is connecting to the base to allow the glue to bond well.

Step 5: Once the ring has been drying upright for around an hour, check the cabochon or cameo is bonding to the base by applying an even pressure with the flat of your thumb. If you hear a lifting sound after you have removed your thumb, you may need to apply a touch more glue. You can do this by sliding a toothpick underneath the

your cameo or cabochon to adhere to. If the base is already textured, inspect it to see if it has enough bond points to allow the cabochon or cameo to stick well. If a base is too textured, with many bumps or too curved, it will be difficult for the glue to adhere correctly and will result in your ring breaking.

Step 3: Once you have prepared the surface of the ring, gather the glue, cameo or cabochon and toothpick together. Add a thin layer of glue to the surface of the ring base frame and also to the back of the cameo or cabochon using the toothpick. You can use the flat-nosed pliers to gently hold the cameo or cabochon while you apply the glue with the toothpick to avoid getting any adhesive on your fingers.

Step 4: Use a piece of plasticine to hold the ring upright by sticking it to a flat

Choose a ring base to suit your cabochon or cameo.

Add texture to the back of the cameo.

Apply a thin layer of adhesive to the back of the cameo.

Use pliers to manoeuvre the cabochon into place.

Check the cameo is starting to adhere by pressing down firmly.

Use pliers to gently push down the frame's caging fronds.

cameo or cabochon and levering upwards. If the cabochon or cameo gives resistance and is not lifted easily then it has bonded correctly, should be left to dry and won't need any more glue.

Step 6: Leave the ring to dry upright for twenty-four hours before wearing to give the glue a chance to dry. Once the ring has dried fully, remove from the plasticine base and check that the size has not been altered during the making process by mistake. If it has, readjust again until it fits correctly. If the ring base you're using has caging fronds, these should be pushed down to enclose the cameo or cabochon. This will give a professional finish and prevent the fronds from catching on clothing or skin.

Tutorial 2: Gold Insect Hat Pin

It is easy to make something beautiful out of something that people may not think is necessarily appealing. Take insects: most people tend to frown upon them and think that they are disgusting, horrid or not something you should be wearing upon your person. Steampunk often uses bugs in a metaphorical way. Take the humble cockroach – it is said that it can live through a nuclear blast and for weeks without a head. Steampunk, being a post-apocalyptic-influenced genre, borrows heavily from this ideal and provides the metaphor for the underdog making good. Insects, beetles and bugs are given a mechanical makeover with this tutorial and I will be showing you how to work with plastic or rubber insects and using paint to turn the bugs into decorative items for a hat or scarf.

For this tutorial you will need:
Spray paint in a metallic shade

Gold insect hat pin.

3–5 flat-backed gems in a colour of
  your choice
1–2 cogs or watch parts
Large decorative pin with a flat base
  area
1 large or 2 small toy insects

Tools:
Strong jewellery adhesive
Flat-nosed pliers

Toothpicks
Scrap cardboard or plastic
Plasticine (optional)

Step 1: Take the one large or two small bugs and begin the preparation of getting them ready to paint. Make sure the bugs are clean and have no residue on them. If the bugs are greasy at all, which can sometimes happen if they are

1

Prepare the insect for painting.

2

Spray the bug with paint until completely covered on both sides.

3

Leave the insect to dry and gather together your other materials.

4

Glue the bug to the pin back and leave to dry.

5

Test out the placement for the gems and cogs before gluing into place.

6

Glue all of the gems into place and leave to dry before wearing.

made from rubber, use some warm water with a few drops of washing-up liquid to clean them thoroughly. Once washed, leave the bugs to air dry or towel until completely dry.

Step 2: Once dry, place the bug onto a disposable sheet of cardboard or plastic, ready to be painted. Protect the surrounding area from any potential spray back and ideally spray your bug outdoors to minimize the inhalation of the paint. Always wear a protective mask when using spray paints. Shake the spray paint for a good two to three minutes to allow the paint to be well mixed and ready to use. Spray the paint onto a piece of cardboard for a second to clear the nozzle and allow the fresh paint to be released without obstruction. Position the spray with the base of the can facing to the floor and begin to spray the bug at a distance of thirty centimetres (one foot) with slow back and forth movements until it is completely covered. Once you have a thin coating, leave the paint until it is touch dry. Once the paint has been left to dry for at least ten minutes, turn the bug over and spray until the underside is equally covered. When spraying, you will be able to cover the bug quickly, so to avoid dripping paint make sure you stop as soon as the original colour of the bug has disappeared from sight. It is better to stop too quickly and have to cover the bug again than to spray for too long and potentially end up with unsightly paint runs or blobs.

Step 3: Leave the bug to dry for another twenty minutes and then repeat the previous step, paying close attention to cover spaces which may have been missed, such as the sides and any nooks and crannies between antennae, legs or wings. Leave the paint to dry completely for at least six hours to avoid chipping or scratching from handling.

Step 4: Take the hat pin and hold the bug over the base to distinguish which area of the bug is the flattest and most suitable for gluing. Prepare the base by making sure it is clean and has texture to allow the glue to bond sufficiently. Take the jewellery adhesive and put a large dab – around a pea-sized lump should be sufficient – on the base of the bug. Also place a thin spreading of glue onto the surface of the pin using a toothpick. Use the toothpick to spread the glue on the bug in a circle, reflecting the size of the pin base. Press both the bug and the base together firmly. Should there be any glue spilling when squeezing the two items together, use a piece of cardboard or another toothpick to gently wipe away the excess. Pay special attention to wiping the glue downwards and away from the bug to avoid getting any of it on the front of the piece. Jewellery adhesive can be difficult to remove and can stain some paints white. Leave the pin to dry for twenty-four hours to allow the glue to set solidly.

Step 5: Select the gems, cogs or watch parts you would like to adorn your insect and try out placements on the insect. You can use gems to recover some of the details of the anatomy on the bug you may have lost when coating it in paint, such as the eyes or wing tips. The gems should be used to enhance the bug and not as the main focal point, so avoid making them into a design but use them more as accents. Once you have selected where you would like to place your gems, lay the pin flat and, if needs be, secure with a piece of plasticine underneath to stop it moving.

Step 6: When you're happy with your placement of the gems and cogs, you can begin to glue them into place. Select a gem and use a toothpick to add a small dab of glue on the back. Manoeuvre into place with the glued toothpick but be

careful not to use the wet end to touch the top of the jewel as this may cause it to discolour. Press down with the dry end of the toothpick to bond the gem with the surface of the bug. Repeat this step for each gem, cog or watch part. Once all the decorative elements are in place, leave to dry for a further twenty-four hours before wearing.

Tutorial 3: Simple Feather and Cog Brooch

Feathers and cogs go brilliantly together as they provide a contrasting design coupling: mechanics with nature, hard with soft, delicate with rough. Using contrasting materials keeps a design fresh and unpredictable, which in turn creates an interesting, unique item. For this tutorial you will need a small amount of fabric – a fabric scrap from another project will be fine. This is to make a base for your brooch to add softness and continuity to link the two design elements. You will also need three medium-sized feathers or six small feathers. These feathers should be long wing feathers and not feathers from the body as they will contain too much down which will stick to the glue and make the finished product look messy. If the feathers you choose have a downy base, be sure to trim away the excess fluffy parts, known as the afterfeather, from the hollow shaft and just leave the top, smoother barb. Once you have trimmed the feathers and cleared away any excess down, you're ready to begin.

You can use this brooch to decorate anything you wish, such as a corset, jacket or even a bag.

For this tutorial you will need:
3 medium-sized wing feathers or 6 small feathers
Small piece of fabric, preferably felt
Brooch pin or back
3–6 cogs in various sizes

Feather and cog brooch.

Tools:
Hot glue gun and glue sticks
Scissors
Pen

Step 1: Plug in the glue gun to heat up. While the glue gun is heating up, arrange the feathers so they are grouped together in a bunch. Take the scrap of fabric and roll the feathers into it from the bottom edge, covering the shafts. Make sure the fabric covers the tips completely. If the fabric doesn't reach completely round the shaft of the feathers, try a larger scrap of fabric. Turn the fabric over to the side that you don't want to face outwards and draw a bird foot – a three-pronged-type shape – onto it, making sure the extended 'claws' will cover the bare part of the feathers. The claw parts of the material will be used to point up and away from the shaft of the feathers.

Step 2: When you're happy that the material is the correct size and that the shape will cover the exposed parts of the feathers, very carefully use the scissors to cut out the shape. When cutting out the shape, you should use the scissors to make long fluid cuts and avoid making a series of small cuts, as this will make a ragged edge on the material. Take particular care when cutting out the claw shapes as these will be fairly intricate to manoeuvre around. Once

Sketch out a claw shape onto the fabric.

Add a thin layer of glue to the fabric and wrap around the feathers, pinching together.

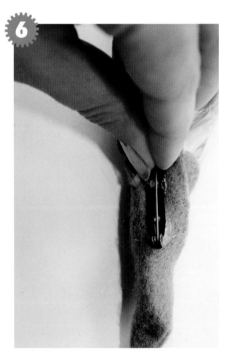

Cut out the pattern from the material.

Use the glue gun to apply the adornments onto the material.

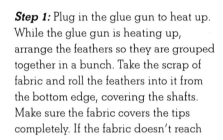

Glue the feathers together.

Attach the brooch back to the material using the glue gun.

you have cut the shape out, set it to one side, ready to be used later.

Step 3: Check that the glue gun is heated up to an appropriate temperature. Take the feathers in their bunch, making sure the shafts are at an even length and touching. Manipulate the feathers until they are in a tiered formation to add depth and interest to the design. Once you're happy with the layering of the feathers, add glue to the inside of each shaft and press together. Don't apply any glue to the outside of the shafts as this is where you will be adding the material. Leave for one to two minutes to allow the glue to dry before moving on to the next step.

Step 4: Take the fabric and add a thin line of glue around the whole of the outside edge using the glue gun. Glue gun adhesive dries quickly so make sure you adhere the edges of the material at speed to prevent this from happening. Place the feathers in the centre of the fabric and roll up till the edge is sealed all the way round. Pinch the fabric together from the bottom to the top, paying special attention to the edges to allow the glue to permeate the fabric. Leave to dry for one to two minutes and then gently pull on the fabric to test that it has adhered correctly. If the fabric pulls away, re-apply glue to the outside edge and pinch together again until you're satisfied that it has strongly adhered.

Step 5: Gather together the cogs and watch parts you would like to use and place them onto the fabric at the bottom of the feathers. Try different ways of placing where you would like the cogs to sit. The cogs should be used as a simple adornment for your design and not be too overpowering in number or placement. Once you have decided on a placement for the pieces, add a dab of glue to the back of each piece and press down in sequence. Be careful when adding the glue to the metal pieces as they will conduct the heat from the adhesive and can scald your fingers. To protect your fingers, hold the cogs with a pair of pliers and press down onto the fabric. Once you have sequentially added the cogs, lay the piece flat and leave to dry for a further five minutes.

Step 6: Turn the feathers over so the cogs are facing downwards. Locate the best area for your brooch pin to sit. You need to bear in mind which way you would like your brooch positioned – facing with the feather tips upwards or downwards, to the left or right – and make sure the pin is in the correct place to facilitate this. When you have located the ideal spot, add a medium to large stripe of glue from the gun to the fabric and use pliers to put the brooch back in place. Press down with an even pressure on either end of the brooch and leave to dry for an hour until completely dry. Once you have finished your brooch, pin it to your favourite jacket, bag or corset.

Chapter 6
Headgear

Never look backwards or you'll fall down the stairs.
– RUDYARD KIPLING

Millinery is a wonderful way of using a basic item to create a specific style or look. Hats throughout history have demonstrated a variety of uses from pure decoration, such as beautiful Easter bonnets and debonair top hats, to functional and protective service helmets and military wear. Wealth and riches, status and power have commonly been associated with types of hats, particularly in the Victorian and Edwardian eras. Even today, hats are sometimes used to exhibit one's social standing. For example, some horse-racing events across the UK still have a day dedicated to showing off elaborate hats, the more over the top the better.

In Steampunk there are a handful of millinery designs that are used as bases to build on. These bases are classic blueprints of millinery, such as the top and tricorn hat, but usually half the size. This reduction in the size of the design adds a touch of whimsy, which is integral to the tongue-in-cheek nature of Steampunk style. Most small-sized hats can be purchased as ready-made items but will require some customization to make them into something special. There is an option to create smaller hats

yourself but this can be challenging for a beginner; however, with practice and over time, you should be able to make these well and to a high standard. A top hat is one of the easier designs to replicate and can be made by using cardboard tubes and fabric covering. There are some patterns online that are easy to follow for smaller hats, but you should try and discover your own ways of making these to practise your skills.

Crafting your own unique headgear will teach you a multitude of fresh techniques that will be transferable to any future projects you might wish to undertake. Through making your own hats you will really gain a sense of what is possible within larger projects and it will give you a chance to experiment with a plethora of materials and techniques.

Fascinators can range from very simple quick projects that can take under an hour to create to large headpieces that will require immense skill and many hours, if not days, to complete. It is important that you practise your new-found skills as much as possible when it comes to hat-making as the more pieces you complete, the

more accomplished your skills will become. Try using a variety of different materials as this will make your fascinators unique and interesting to others as well as keep your skill set evolving.

When looking around for inspiration, try researching historical headdresses, hats and other headgear to see how people throughout the ages created them. This will give your designs authentic historical reference but will also make them more individual. Sometimes headgear can look impossible to replicate, but try to view items with a technical and searching eye. What has served as a base for the hat, was fabric used to connect pieces, has it been sewn to a band or glued to a base? Look really closely and study the pieces to get a feel for how they may have been created.

Try replicating a historical item such as a bonnet or hat and add some Steampunk flair to it. This will provide you with an instant base to work from and will help you to skillfully manipulate ideas and transpose them into reality. Fascinators should work with the shape of the head and complement, not

LEFT: Steampunk headdress by Devine Delinquents. (Charis Talbot Photography)

distract from, the wearer. Some hats and fascinators can be overpowering, giving too much focus on the headgear and not on the rest of the outfit. Try theming your fascinator into an outfit as this will provide continuity and make an ensemble seem well thought out and polished.

Some materials will be more historically accurate than others, so when choosing items to add to headgear, research what was available from the time period and replicate these as best you can. However, don't be afraid to throw in a modern twist if you feel this would work with your design.

Victorian hats were usually made from starched heavy fabric and many featured jewel and glass bead embellishments. Flappers of the 1920s wore long ostrich feathers attached to fabric bands adorned with crystal and glass sparkling beads. Hats from the 1930s and '40s were often small pillbox versions and very demure in design, usually made from felt or wool. Hats from the 1950s onwards became larger and more overstated so aren't ideal for a specific historical reference, but you may wish to research these designs to make a more retro version.

If creating headgear with a futuristic twist, try teaming historic design elements together with modern materials such as plastic, foam or glitter. The materials chosen should be far enough apart in their respective timescales to make them instantly recognizable as modern or historical but not be so unrelated that they look disparate. Whichever items you choose to use, you will more than likely be able to theme them well using colour, size and shape.

Items used to create fascinators work best when grouped together using length, height and symmetry, a similar idea to that of flower arranging. Arranging items in terms of size, length or shape makes it easier to create a

design based on a structural framework, adding architecture to the piece. Once you have a structurally sound shape, you can begin to add in design ideas which work for your piece. This will create a fascinator that is altogether better thought out and combines a strong design with a great idea.

For quick and easy fascinator-making, you can buy pre-made bases which you can build upon and add decorative items to. These will save you time but they won't save you money as they can be quite expensive. To make fascinator- and hat-making more affordable you can create many of the base elements yourself. It is far cheaper to use transferable materials such as cardboard and plastic to make hat bases. Through making your own fascinator and hat bases, you will not only save money but also create something entirely unique.

With headgear, it is important to consider weight and unwieldiness, as it is not ideal to be constantly having to adjust a headpiece that won't stay in its correct position or have it knocking on every single door frame you walk through. As a rule, it makes sense to keep headpieces as light as possible. This may mean getting creative with the items you use on your fascinator. Fabric, feathers, artificial flowers and foam are good components to use, whereas heavy items and fabrics like leather and metal can weigh your piece down. There are plenty of sufficient lightweight replicas of heavier items that you can purchase or you can recreate with other lighter materials. For example, chains are often available in plastic; try the local hardware store and use spray paint to change the colour. Metal items can be recreated in polymer clay and painted with metallic paints to replicate many different Steampunk items such as padlocks or keys. Plastic chains are not suitable bases for jewellery-making due to their fragility but are great for

decoration on headgear, with the upside being that you can paint them in a colour to complement your project.

Polystyrene shapes are also ideal for fascinators. There are many different ways to use polystyrene shapes: wrapping them in synthetic hair, covering them in glitter, or painting them. The available range of shapes has become more diverse in the last few years and there are now many viable pieces on the market. These shapes can be attached to headbands and decorated with artificial flowers, materials and other accoutrements. Polystyrene can be added to headbands by using wire and craft glues. Hot glue can cause polystyrene to melt so it is best avoided and substituted for a cold-set craft glue.

Simple Fascinator Tutorial

A simple fascinator should feature a minimal design and be used to add an accent to an updo. In Steampunk there are no hard and fast rules when it comes to hairstyles, but a simple updo is an easy go-to style when you wish to achieve an exciting look with minimal effort. For most, a simple chignon accented with a simple fascinator will make an outfit and take you under ten minutes to create.

When using fascinators, placement is everything. Some people like to place them at the front of the head for maximum effect, whereas others like to use them to simply accent a hairstyle to add simple elegance. When choosing materials, in particular ribbons, grosgrain is an obvious choice because of its advantages over satin or polyester. Grosgrain is thicker and sturdier than its single weave counterparts; it has a stiffness to the fabric due to the double and ribbed weave. This allows the grosgrain to maintain its shape when glued or stitched into place, making it ideal for fascinators. It comes in a multitude of patterns and colours, so is an incredibly versatile material.

To create this piece, carefully follow the steps below and be imaginative, adding your own twist when it comes to selecting colours.

For this tutorial you will need:
Plastic hair comb
2 x 25cm grosgrain ribbon in complementary colours
1 large metal charm
3 small metal charms
3 x 4mm jump rings

Tools:
Hot glue gun
Scissors
Pliers

Step 1: To begin, take the plastic hair comb and work out where it sits best on your head. The comb should sit flush to the head with around one and a half inches of hair either side. This is to allow room for the extended ribbon. You should do this in front of a mirror so you are able to see the placement clearly. Once you have found the best and most comfortable place for your comb, check that the ribbon won't extend over the face or stick up too high from the head. Plug in your glue gun to heat up for five minutes. While waiting, cut two lengths of grosgrain ribbon, one an inch longer than the other, and seal the ends with a lighter to prevent them from fraying.

Step 2: Fold the cut pieces of ribbon in half and overlap the join at the ends. Make sure the join is at the centre and back of the ribbon and glue into place. Use a line of glue on one of the ribbon ends and press down; repeat the step with the other end, taking care to avoid scalding yourself with the glue. Repeat the step with the other piece of ribbon.

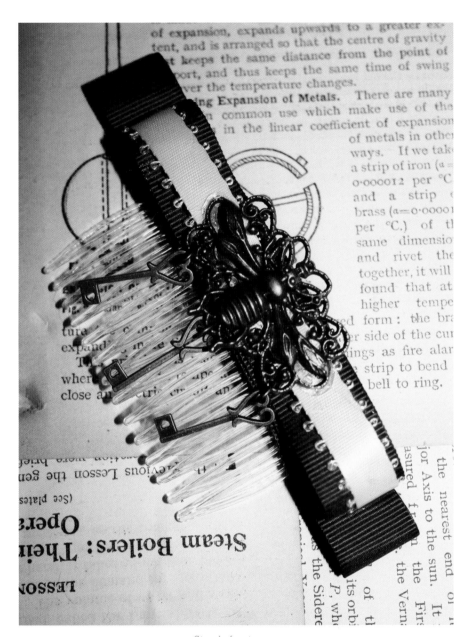

Simple fascinator.

Take the plastic comb and lay the larger ribbon facing downwards with the join facing up. Lay the plastic comb onto the ribbon with the teeth facing downwards and the top concave edge touching the centre line of the ribbon. Before gluing, hold the comb up and check that it's facing the right way and will sit correctly in your chosen spot. When you are satisfied, add a fairly thick line of glue to the top of the comb, on the top strip only, taking care not to get any glue on the teeth. Very quickly place the ribbon onto the comb and press down by sliding your fingers underneath the larger ribbon loop.

Step 3: Take the metal charm and add the three smaller hanging charms to the underneath. Open the three jump rings and hook through the loops on the underside of the charm. Close the jump rings using pliers or cat claw clippers. If your charm doesn't have anywhere to add hanging charms, you can add a line of chain through the large charm's main connector ring and hang the smaller charms from there. You may need to extend the chain to the edges of the charm to make the smaller charms hang correctly. Set to one side for inclusion later.

Step 4: Take the smaller looped ribbon and use it to measure a same-sized piece of thinner decorative ribbon in a contrasting colour to wrap around its centre. When you're happy with the length of the thinner ribbon, cut and seal the end with a lighter. Take the thin ribbon and place around the centre of the larger loop lengthways, taking care to make sure it's not too taut as this will cause the ribbon underneath to bend and not sit correctly. Place the ends of the thinner ribbon together at the back of the larger ribbon and make sure it runs equally around the centre of the larger ribbon. Once you're happy with the placement of the thinner ribbon, use the glue gun to place a thin strip of glue around the centre of the larger ribbon. Be sparing with your use of glue and press down hard to make sure the ribbons adhere well to each other; this will prevent the glue bleeding through the fabric. Leave the loop to dry for a few minutes before moving on to the next step. This will prevent you from accidentally nudging the centre ribbon out of place.

Step 5: Take the plastic comb with the

larger ribbon loop on it and also the smaller ribbon loop. Place the smaller ribbon loop on top of the larger bottom ribbon. A central placement will be preferable to make the piece even on either side. Use the hot glue gun to

Cut two lengths of ribbon and seal the ends with a lighter.

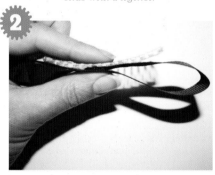

Glue the larger piece of ribbon into a loop and adhere to the plastic comb.

Add hanging charms to your centrepiece using jump rings.

Cut the thinner ribbon and glue together.

Glue the two ribbons together.

Attach the charm to the centre of the bows.

Reshape the bow and tidy any loose glue strands away before wearing.

secure the bow by adding a medium amount of glue to the middle of the smaller loop at the join. Press the loop down onto the larger loop and hold in place for a few minutes until dry and secure.

Step 6: Take the large charm and place on the centre of the smaller bow until you have a placement you're happy with. Check when placing the charm that it will be fully supported by the fabric underneath when glued and won't fall forward. If you think the charm won't adhere to the bow correctly, you may need to create some extra support on the centre of the bow to counteract the weight of the piece. You could do this by adding another bow or a ribbon flower, which is quite easy to make by folding small loops of fabric and gluing at the centre. When you're happy that the charm will sit correctly, take the glue gun and add a medium to large blob of glue on its underside. Press down firmly on the charm and hold in place using a tea towel or piece of fabric to avoid scalding your fingers on the hot glue. Wipe away any excess glue with a scrap of fabric, avoiding smearing onto the surrounding ribbon.

Step 7: When the ribbon is attached to the comb, leave for at least an hour to dry before wearing and be sure to clean off any excess glue strands by gently pulling or peeling them away. Reshape the bow by running your fingers in between the loops to puff it back up; this can be done between wears to keep the shape.

Try wearing the comb with different hairstyles and with different outfits. As this piece is versatile and fairly small, it will make a statement without being overbearing. Why not try making a piece to match an everyday work outfit in coordinating colours using a similar pattern?

Medium Fascinator Tutorial

Now you have made one fascinator, it should be relatively easy to progress to this next piece. However, do set aside a decent amount of time as it can take a little while to complete. You may wish to split this tutorial into two sections to

make it more manageable.

You will need to create your own base for this piece, so you need to be mindful of your ideal end design and plan your materials and items carefully. When creating your mood board consider your final piece and then take one or two

Finished medium fascinator.

design elements away to keep the design streamlined and simple. When designing headgear, you should take into account a few things. Pieces should be designed to fit the curvature of your head and also be able to be styled if you plan to wear them around a certain hairstyle. Particular hairstyles, especially larger coiffed styles, may obscure headdresses or make it difficult to attach them to the head.

The surface area you create for the base of the design should be fairly small so as not to overload the base and make it too heavy or obscured. You may wish to invest in a milliner's block or foam head, as this makes creating headpieces much easier if you plan to make larger designs on a more frequent basis. Don't forget to try on the fascinator as you progress through the steps to make sure it is taking shape with your own head, but remember to check that any glues you may have used are dry before you do so.

If you wish, and where possible, you can always stitch items onto your base using a heavy gauge needle. This will make your fascinator very sturdy and hard-wearing, but it will be more time-consuming to create if you choose this method over gluing. Not all materials will suit stitching, however, and it should be avoided for metals, polystyrene and latex.

For this tutorial you will need:
15–20 feathers in various sizes and
   colours
25cm millinery netting
Large barrette clip
50cm satin ribbon
50cm velvet ribbon
50cm lace trim
Wooden laser-cut pendant

Tools:
Hot glue gun
Scissors

Lighter
Dressmaking pins

Step 1: Prepare the feathers by arranging them on the flat part of the barrette. Consider which feathers you would like to be more visible and prominent at the front of the design and choose some eye-catching, nicely shaped pieces to feature. Feathers should be tiered, with longer feathers towards the back and smaller feathers towards the front. Avoid placing feathers that are a similar length next to each other as this will create a solidly tiered look which will look stunted and won't flow with the shape of the head. Try alternating longer feathers with slightly shorter feathers to create a softer look, replicating that of a bird's wing. Once you have the feathers placed in your preferred position, take a photograph or make a sketch to note their position before moving on to the next step so you can refer back to it later.

Step 2: The centrepiece of the fascinator will be a large double bow that will span the whole length of the barrette. This can be made with two lengths of satin ribbon in a colour of your choice. Consider the Steampunk colour palette of neutral, cream or taupe for the base element of the bow. Choose a bolder coloured stripe for the outside of the bow as this will contrast well with the base. To make the double bow, first measure the length of the barrette on top of the satin ribbon to gauge the length. Allow the ribbon to hang over the edge of the barrette by approximately an inch. Mark the ribbon with a pin at this point to keep a reminder and, without cutting, measure the same length again and then cut at the end. Use a lighter to seal either end of the length of ribbon.

Step 3: For the smaller part of the bow, lay the ribbon flat next to the pre-cut

piece and measure a second shorter piece. The second piece of ribbon should be cut two inches shorter than the original piece. Once cut, seal the ends of the ribbon with a lighter to avoid fraying. Cut the same lengths of the

Arrange the feathers into your preferred position on the barrette.

Cut and seal the lengths of ribbon.

Cut a second piece of ribbon along with a length of velvet and lace trim.

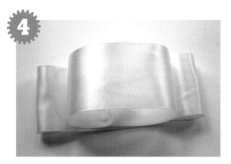

Glue both pieces of ribbon into separate loops.

Glue the wooden pendant to the centre of the bow.

Glue the netting to the barrette.

Glue the velvet and the lace around the smaller loop.

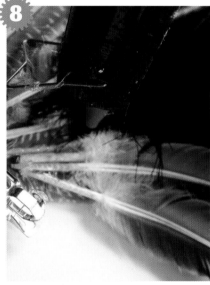

Glue the feathers onto the barrette.

Glue the bow on top of the feathers and netting and hold in place till dry.

Glue the two loops together to make the large bow.

Trim and glue the netting.

velvet ribbon and the lace trim to match the two pieces of satin ribbon. Seal the ends of the velvet ribbon with a lighter but don't do the same to the lace trim as it won't fray when wearing and will melt if touched with a flame. To make the lace trim tidy on the ends, cut through a section that is not part of the main pattern.

Step 4: Plug the glue gun in and wait for it to heat up. While waiting, fold the longest piece of satin ribbon in half and place the ends in the centre. When the glue is ready, squeeze a thin strip of adhesive onto one end of the ribbon, leaving a centimetre from each edge, and place the other end of the ribbon over the top of the glue. Squeeze down gently, being careful not to scald your fingers on the glue to join the ends together. Repeat the same step with the smaller piece of satin ribbon and leave both loops to dry for five minutes until the hot glue has set.

Step 5: To create the contrasting ribbon stripe around the bow, wrap the ribbon around the outside of the bow so it sits around the middle circumference of the material. Start with the velvet ribbon, glue at the back of the satin ribbon, paying special attention not to spill any glue onto the velvet as it will mark easily with heat. Once glued, repeat the step with the lace trim. Layer the lace trim, running it around the circumference of the velvet ribbon. Check the lace trim to make sure it is sitting correctly, running flat and not folded at any points. Once you're happy with the positioning, keep the ribbon slightly taught and glue the trim into place at the same point as the other ribbons. Repeat the same step for the smaller ribbon. Leave to dry for at least five minutes until the glue has set.

Step 6: To attach the two bows together, place the smaller bow on top of the larger one and adjust until they're layered with an even amount of fabric on either side of the barrette. When you're happy with the placement, lift the smaller bow and place a line of glue at the centre point, on top of the larger bow, and press together. Leave to dry for a few minutes then repeat, gluing on either side of the underside on the smaller bow, making sure it is firmly adhered. Once the glue is dry, move on to the next step.

Step 7: Take the wooden laser-cut pendant and place in the mid-centre of the bow and check that the placement is perfect and central. Check all the way around the bow to make sure the accenting velvet ribbon is level and central around the circumference of both bows, along with the lace trim. When satisfied the bows are equal, level and successfully adhered, glue the pendant onto the mid-centre of the bow and hold in place until the glue has dried to an acceptable level. This should take a few minutes. If the glue doesn't adhere well to begin with, remove the pendant and clean away any dried glue before adding another fresh amount of adhesive and repeating the same step.

Step 8: Set the bow to one side and gather the feathers, barette and sketch or photograph of the layout that you made earlier. Lay the feathers out in the order you will require them to be glued to the barrette, remembering to start with the back layer first. Begin to dab a medium amount of glue on each part of the feather shaft that will be in contact with the barrette and, in turn, press them onto the front of the barrette and hold still until the glue dries. Layer the feathers one by one and shape into a wing shape. If some feathers are not sitting correctly or if you run out of room along the length of the barrette, begin to layer behind the barrette. Layer upwards onto the shafts of the other feathers. Continue to glue each feather individually and build up until you have the shape you like. Keep adding glue to the shafts on the reverse of the structure until the feathers feel secure and are firmly in place. You may need to add glue over the backs of the shafts to create a layer of adhesive which will dry solid, making the structure firm and sturdy.

Step 9: Take the millinery netting and fold in half so the cut ends meet. Keep the netting in a 'U' shape and twist at the centre point loosely a few times so that there is a more compacted part on which to apply the glue. Place the twisted part of the netting in the centre front of the barrette, on top of the glued feathers. The netting should point upwards and towards either side of the feathers. Trim the netting until it measures approximately one inch longer than the longest feather on either side. Trim the netting carefully and shape it so it has a clean line to the cut edge. Once the netting is trimmed, remove from the barrette and place a medium circle of hot glue on the reverse centre twist and hold it in place till the glue has dried fully. Repeat the same on the opposite side of the netting, placing a medium dab of glue, and wait until fully dried. The netting should then hold in place without untwisting. Once the glue is dry, set the netting down. If the netting untwists when not being held, add more glue to both sides of the original adhered sites and wait until dry.

Step 10: Once the netting has dried and feels stiff and secure at the centre twist, add a medium to large dab of hot glue to the back and press down onto the centre of the barrette. Hold the netting still by placing your fingers either side of the twist and wait until the glue has dried fully. Be careful not to scald your fingers on the hot glue.

Step 11: The double bow is now ready to be placed as the final finishing touch on the centre of the netting twist and lengthways along the barrette. Apply another dab of glue to hold the bow in place on top of the netting and hold down until dry. Once dry, reshape the bow by running your fingers around the inside of the loops. This will make the bow look fresh and not squashed.

Once your fascinator is complete, leave to dry and the glue to set fully for at least two hours. Store your fascinator by keeping it wrapped inside a silk scarf or similar when it is not being worn. To protect the feathers from being bent or squashed, keep the fascinator inside a shoe or hat box. Hat boxes can be a lovely addition to a wardrobe and add an authentic Victorian feel to any bedroom or dressing table. Antique original Victorian hat boxes can be bought occasionally at flea markets or through online auction websites. Should you wish to make your own, however, you could decorate a modern box with Steampunk-inspired trims and materials.

Art stores sell a variety of plain boxes which can be decoupaged and made beautiful. Department stores which have a millinery area will also be able to advise on the best way to store hats and will often have hat boxes on sale due to them not being as popular as they once were. When storing millinery which features animal products like feathers or delicate fabrics, you should include a few anti-pest devices such as moth balls, or spray the box with an anti-moth spray every now and again.

Chapter 7
Other Accessories

Quiet minds cannot be perplexed or frightened but go on in fortune or misfortune at their own private pace, like a clock during a thunderstorm.
— ROBERT LOUIS STEVENSON

Accessories are an integral part of the overall Steampunk style and can be used to turn an outfit from perfect to spectacular. To enhance and give a cohesive look to an outfit, teaming together accessories is a great way of learning how to see things objectively when designing. If you can master the techniques of making basic accessories, you can unlock an inexpensive way of building on an outfit and making it stand out.

Use your own personal sense of style to create something exclusive and theme it to items you already own to make an outfit that's effortless. Try making a collection of items that match so you have a complete set to use. There will be staple items such as gloves or scarves that you favour wearing, so to allow for a multitude of combinations make plenty of these in different designs, patterns and colours. Accessories are a good way to top off an outfit, and you will find that once you have honed your skills you will not look at putting together an outfit in the same way again.

Paints

To transform an item into a Steampunk creation, most things can be painted using the colour palette of the genre. Colours such as gold, brown, beige, black and metallics are the most popular. Other hues to experiment with can be borrowed from the main influences of Steampunk, for example, post-apocalyptic colours evoke thoughts of washed-out navy, combat colours such as khaki, or red clay. Victorian shades are typically more jewel-like. Jade, amethyst, ruby and sapphire were all popular pigments in the period and were often used to excess in interiors and clothing. Certain colours were more expensive than others due to dyes being partly made from a mixture of natural ingredients that could vary hugely in cost and availability.

In modern times, paints are an easily affordable and readily available way of transforming an item, with low costs involved. Should you wish to take your love of Steampunk to the next level, you could use paint to transform furniture in your house to give it an antique or futuristic look. There are plenty of tutorials on how to create Steampunk-inspired interiors on related internet forums which will give you a wealth of tips and advice. The type of paint you will need for projects varies greatly depending on the type of materials you are using.

I have covered the two main types of paint that are easily available and simple to use. These paints are perfect for many different surfaces and you will therefore not have to give too much thought to the best paint to choose when planning a project. If any of the surfaces you would like to paint on are not covered below, please research suitable paints for your project. If you're not able to find the information you require easily, do not hesitate to ask your local art supplies store, as they will be well versed in suitable products for all types of projects.

Spray paint

Spray paint can be used on a variety of items and materials such as wood, glass, plastic, ceramic, metal and even some fabrics. You can quickly add a coat of paint in just a few minutes using spray paint, whereas traditional brushes and

LEFT: The model wears goggles and ray gun by Devine Delinquents.

Spray paint.

paint pots can take much longer and require a considerable drying time. Spray paint is ideal for coating a large area in a small amount of time and gives a flawless finish, if used correctly.

Spray paint can be used as a base colour when short on time and details can be added in acrylics by using brushes, for example painting filigree or mechanics onto a ray gun. Spray paint can also be used in layers by combining three coats of different colours and sanding back to reveal and expose the shades below. This creates a futuristic and apocalyptic look, particularly if you use metallic shades.

Certain spray paints are made for specific projects, such as glass painting, flooring, car paint and fabrics, amongst other things. There are many different types of spray paint available on the market and they can provide effects such as a stone effect, crackle glazing, high shine chrome amongst others, and these are great for interior projects. Spray paint is available in almost any colour and can be easily purchased at

hardware stores and online. Be aware that some spray paints are not suitable to be worn for prolonged periods of time in close contact with skin. Check the manufacturer's instructions and stick to skin-safe paints for fabrics and jewellery items.

When using spray paint on wood, sand the wood and make sure it is free from any dust before spraying. This will give you an even coat and provide a long-lasting wear. For other materials, clean thoroughly before spraying, using dish soap to clean any grease or debris away. Having a surface that is dirty or greasy will make it difficult for the paint to adhere and could result in the coating being uneven. Not preparing your materials correctly could be costly, as removing spray paint is very difficult, time-consuming and often not even possible.

Always make sure you have enough spray paint to complete a project as it could affect the finish you're trying to achieve if you run out halfway through a coating and it might produce unsightly lines. Be sure to protect the surrounding areas you are working in as spray paint particles do tend to drift and can stain most surfaces they come into contact with. It is best, where possible, to use spray paint outside as this will avoid any damage being caused to your interiors and furnishings. However, outside spaces should be treated with as much care and you should protect surfaces to prevent spraying on patios, grass or similar. Using decorator's sheets, newspaper or tarpaulin will be sufficient to protect areas, but they should be coverings that you don't mind permanently staining. Always use spray paint in a well ventilated area, wearing a protective mask. If you're unable to go outside, keep pets and children away from the paint to avoid any accidents and keep stored out of reach from minors.

Before painting, shake the paint can vigorously so you can hear a rattling sound. Most cans will tell you on the instructions how long to shake before spraying, but around one minute is usually sufficient. Shaking the can allows the paint to be mixed well and will make sure the spray is even. Test the spray by clearing the nozzle onto the protective surface you have laid down and spray for a few seconds to check that the nozzle is clear. Before committing to spraying the whole item, test the paint in an inconspicuous spot to check it adheres correctly. Leave the test patch to dry and if the paint doesn't adhere correctly, is flaky or patchy, you will need to use a primer spray to pre-coat the item. Once the test patch has dried and you're happy with the coverage, you can then begin to paint the rest of the item. If you're not happy with the coverage, test again once you have applied a primer.

To begin the first coat, hold the can with the base pointing towards the floor at a slight downward facing angle and spray from a distance of around thirty centimetres (one foot) in slightly overlapping lines from left to right; then repeat, spraying from top to bottom. Shake the can regularly while spraying to keep the paint well mixed. Apply several thin coats to the item, leaving sufficient drying time in between, as recommended by the instructions on the can. Once you have completely painted your item, leave for at least twenty-four hours before using, as the paint, even though it may look and feel dry, will not have adhered fully until then.

Once you have discovered the simplicity of spray paint, you will find that it provides an extra time-saving solution to traditional painting and unleashes a range of unlikely materials that could be used for all sorts of different projects.

Acrylic paint

Acrylic paint, a multi-purpose medium, is versatile and can be used on items such as ceramics, metal, plastic and wood, amongst other surfaces. For most projects, craft acrylic is the best choice as it will have a mixed combination of pigment with an adhesive resin such as PVA glue or vinyl. Avoid using vinyl-based acrylics on plastic as the adhesion will not be as long-lasting as PVA-based products. Try searching for products that state they are hard-wearing for projects you know will need to be durable and stand the test of time.

Acrylic paints are easy to apply as they are water soluble when wet. This means that any mistakes at the painting stage can be simply wiped away with a damp cloth. Acrylics set once they're dry, making them water resistant and durable. As acrylic paint is fast-drying, it is a sensible option for coating smaller items. Most acrylic paints, when used in a single thin layer, will dry in one to two hours. They will provide enough coverage of an item to only require one coat.

Acrylics come in a variety of shades but you can also mix them together to create unique hues. Most craft acrylics have ranges of pigments that are incredibly diverse and span a lot of the colour spectrum, making it easy to pick the hues you need straight off the shelf. They come in a variety of product sizes; planning for the correct amount before starting a project is crucial to avoid running out or wasting money by over-compensating.

Primary colours can be purchased in large quantities; it is advisable to buy these staple shades so that they can be mixed to create any hue you wish. Buying white and black is also recommended for lightening or darkening shades.

When painting surfaces, ensure they're clean and grease-free by using dish soap and drying thoroughly. Sand down wood before painting and always test paint on an inconspicuous area before committing to paint the whole piece. Use brushes that are suitable for the coverage you would like to achieve. For example, if you're covering a whole item, use a medium to large brush. For smaller items, scale the brush size down so it suits the size of the line you would like to create. Invest in a small painting kit that has a selection of different sized brushes, an artist's palette and a brush bag to store your brushes correctly. Most of these items can be purchased cheaply but the more you can spend, the better quality the brushes will be and the longer they will last. Cheaper brushes have a tendency to shed hairs onto the painted surface and these can be messy to remove.

Always be sure to thoroughly wash your brushes immediately after you have finished painting, as once the acrylic has dried it is very difficult to remove and they will be ruined. If you're going back to a project and want to avoid washing your brushes in between, you can use plastic wrap to cover the ends, thus preventing them from drying out. Wash your brushes in clean water and dry with some paper towel before leaving to air dry. Once thoroughly dry, store your brushes inside the brush bag.

Basic Sewing Techniques

Learning a few sewing techniques will allow you to quickly create items that will last. Sewing by hand can be a rewarding and invaluable skill and will help you in all aspects of crafting. Learning to sew takes practice but with just a few techniques, such as tacking or basting, running stitch and knowing how to create strong, lasting stitches, you can repair items, customize any form of fabric and give broken items a new lease of life. The techniques listed are designed to be learnt in a short amount of time and usable straight away.

To practise basic stitches, you will

Acrylic paints.

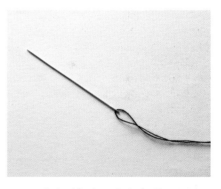

A double-threaded needle.

Top line: running stitch; middle line: tacking stitch; bottom line: back stitch.

need a simple Sharps needle pack consisting of around five needles that vary in thickness. A leather needle is also invaluable as it can be used to stitch thicker, more robust materials. It's good practice when you're learning to use a thimble or some form of protection for your fingers as it's possible to injure yourself without it. Leather needles in particular sometimes have small blades on the end to cut through the fabric easily, which can cause nasty wounds, so it is important to protect yourself. As you practise, you will learn which stitches work best for which projects. Try using a variety of stitches within one project to practise your techniques.

Running stitch

A basic running stitch is possibly the most versatile and easy stitch to learn in sewing and provides a quick way to join fabrics together. Running stitch will hold most light- to moderate-weight fabrics together for posterity. For example, a cotton material will hold very well with a running stitch, whereas a heavy material like denim or leather will require stronger stitches. A single strand of heavy duty cotton thread will suffice for most lightweight projects.

Running stitch is a tight, closely spaced line of stitches measuring approximately one to three millimetres in length. Running stitch is as it sounds – a stitch that is quick to complete. It runs along a hem or can join together two pieces of fabric; it can be used to ruche fabrics or for most quick stitching needs.

To make a running stitch use a doubled-up thread which is knotted at the end and pass the needle from one side of the fabric through to the other. Pull upwards until the knot stops at the back of the fabric. Now weave the needle in and out of each side of the fabric so you create a snake-like stitch. When you have finished a line of

stitches, push the needle through to the back of the fabric and tie a knot in the thread, next to the fabric. Snip off the excess thread behind the knot while holding the needle.

Tacking or basting

Tacking stitch, also known as basting, can be used as a temporary bond and consists of widely spaced loose stitches which will hold fabrics until a more permanent stitch can be applied. Tacking is often used in the fashion and textiles industry to test two different fabrics together before sewing them with a machine. Basting is a good option for testing out trims or embellishments on items such as gloves, corsets and t-shirts. Basting stitch can be easily removed by cutting through the stitches once you have decided what you would like to decorate an item with. It is therefore ideal for holding fabrics together if you're not able to visualize a design in your head. If you begin to create items for others, this stitch is also useful for mocking up designs to preview before committing to a final piece.

To make a tack stitch, thread the needle with a single thread and a knot at the end. Make a large running stitch, pushing the needle through the fabric from one side to the other in a slalom style. Tacking doesn't need to be straight or tidy as it is only temporary.

Strong stitches: back stitch

For a more secure stitch that is guaranteed to last, it is best to use a double thread of heavy duty cotton. This will ensure your stitches will stay in place and hold your materials together. Stronger stitches can also be used to hold unconventional materials together. For example, chains, feathers, dried flowers, can all be sewn onto accessories

Back view of running, tacking and back stitch.

using stronger stitches. This is an alternative method to using glues, meaning your project is wearable straight after you have completed it with no waiting time needed for glue to dry. Stitching should be made invisible on most projects unless you are using it to create a design feature on your finished article. Threads should match, as near as possible, the colour of the fabric you are using, unless you wish to create a contrasting element to your piece. Stitching can be used in a beautiful yet functional way to enhance a design and, if being deliberately used to add flair, should be contrasting or complementary so as to make a bold statement.

Cotton threads are the easiest to use as they're durable, available in almost any colour and versatile for almost all fabric-based projects. Invisible thread, a clear fishing wire-type thread, can be used when stitches are unavoidably prominent on a project. This type of thread should only be used on heavy duty materials as it will ruche and pucker lighter fabrics.

Back stitching will add a strong seam and hold together simple projects like gloves for posterity if done correctly. To back stitch, first thread the needle in the usual fashion and tie a knot in the end. Begin to stitch from the bottom corner of your fabric towards the top. Put the needle through the fabric and pull through, upwards, till the knot stops the thread. Put the needle back through the fabric about half a centimetre along and pull down. Put the needle through the fabric again, half a centimetre to the right, and pull through. Push the needle back through the fabric again about half a centimetre to the left of the original stitch. Continue along the line, putting the needle through the fabric next to the last stitch to the right and ending up one stitch ahead to your left. The stitch should look like a close running stitch along the front of your fabric and an overlapping basting stitch on the back.

Gauntlets and Gloves

Gloves throughout history have been used in all manner of ways: decorative and ceremonial, as protection from the elements, preventing the spread of disease, and for hard work, to name just a few. During the Victorian era, the wearing of gloves was the epitome of high fashion. Women would often be able to make a matching pair of gloves from offcuts of discarded fabric from their large, intricately made dresses. However, this was not the case for ladies higher up the social scale. As elaborate as millinery in the late 1800s, gloves required skilled people to create them and glove-making became a booming industry catering for the Victorians who could afford them.

It was considered, particularly for women, uncouth to be seen with bare hands and different gloves were provided for everyday wear. These were practical, short and made from leather. Evening-wear gloves were long, elbow-length designs made of fabric, which remained popular for black tie dress up until the 1970s when they dropped out of favour. It is no wonder that Steampunk has taken this element of prominent Victorian fashion and repurposed it, as gloves and gauntlets

Finished gauntlets featuring two different designs.

were such a prevalent garment at the time and are synonymous with the period. Gauntlets can be worn layered over longer gloves for extra warmth; or adapt normal gloves by removing the fingers and sewing down the hem to avoid fraying.

Gloves and gauntlets are defined as two different accessories, but both cover the palm and/or the fingers. Gauntlets are short, fingerless gloves, which are usually only worn as a decorative item and normally have a decorative or flared cuff around the wrist. Gloves are usually made to cover the whole hand to just below the wrist.

As gloves can be difficult to make, I have provided a simple technique to customize a ready-made pair. The gauntlets can be made from scratch with

Gauntlets made from latex with a silk bow by Devine Delinquents.

very little material, and the easy pattern is perfect for practising your sewing techniques on. Try using different materials to create gloves and gauntlets and add plenty of decoration to make them unique to your own style.

For this tutorial you will need:
50cm of fabric in a colour or pattern of your choice
Reel of cotton thread that nearest matches the colour of your fabric
Decorations such as buttons, lace or trims

Tools:
Sharps needle in a size suitable for the weight of your fabric
Scissors
Gauntlet pattern

Step 1: To prepare your chosen fabric, first iron it (if it is heat resistant) on the reverse to make it easy to cut the pattern out evenly. It is best to choose a fabric that doesn't require hemming such as jersey or lace. If you have chosen a fabric which doesn't require ironing, skip this step and move straight on to marking your pattern. Once your fabric is ironed and free of any creases, trace the pattern provided and appropriately size to the measurements of your own hands. The pattern featured is suitable for medium-sized hands and should fit most people. If you have trouble finding gloves to fit correctly, be that too big or too small, you can reduce or enlarge the pattern by moving the edges outwards for larger and inwards for smaller and do the same widthways, extending or reducing from the centre line. To get the exact measurement of your hand, measure around the widest centre part of your palm. Extend or reduce the pattern by the difference in measurement. If you're unsure if the pattern is the correct size, trace onto tracing paper and cut out, place onto your hand and check it

fits. Bear in mind that tracing paper will not have any stretch to it and may not completely reach around your hand. This is not to say that the fabric won't fit once it is cut; as long as the paper isn't wildly off fitting around your hand then the cut-out fabric should fit with no problems.

Step 2: Once you have your pattern prepared, you can begin to mark your fabric. There are two methods to try: trace around a card pattern straight onto the fabric using chalk or a disappearing ink pattern pen, or draw onto paper to create a pattern then pin this to your fabric and cut around it. If you're fairly confident that you won't make a mistake when marking the pattern, you can use a plain black ballpoint pen. If you choose to use a ballpoint pen, your fabric should be a darker shade and not too light as the resulting mark may show through on the reverse. Once you have drawn out your pattern once, repeat again for the second gauntlet. If you're using patterned fabric, remember to trace the second pattern facing the same way as the first if you want the two gloves to match exactly.

Step 3: Once you have drawn the pattern onto the fabric, start to cut the fabric out using scissors. Cut in a continuous line and avoid making small scissor cuts to make the pattern smooth. When you have cut out both gloves, turn the fabric so it is inside out and pin together around the edges, making sure to leave gaps at the fingers, thumb hole and wrist. Unravel around a metre of thread in a colour to match the fabric. The stitching will be mostly hidden on this piece so getting an exact match for the thread is not too important. Thread the needle and double it over so the two loose ends are equal and the needle hangs in the 'U' shape. Tie the two ends together by looping the needle around

two fingers. Pass the needle underneath the loop and back over again. Pull the needle away from you and the thread towards you. This will create a tight knot. For some fabrics, you may need a larger knot to stop it slipping through a larger weave. This can be created by repeating the same step above and pulling the knot down when tying so it creates a series of combined knots. If you have chosen a fabric that needs hemming, run a half a centimetre hem around the outside of the two pieces of fabric using a running stitch. This will keep the edges in place and prevent fraying.

Step 4: Take one pinned glove and begin sewing along the outside edge from the wrist to the thumb hole. Use back stitch to keep the seams held together and finish each line of stitches with a knot to avoid them coming undone afterwards. Take time when stitching and make sure you stop stitching at the opening for the thumb.

Step 5: Begin sewing the other side of the thumb hole until you reach the finger end of the pattern. Finish the stitched line with a knot to keep the stitches secure. Now your gauntlet should resemble the shape you require. Try on the glove to check it fits well; if it does you won't need to make any adjustments. If there are areas which could be improved, use pins to mark the points to take in and stitch those adjustments into place. Repeat step 5 and 6 for the second glove.

Step 6: Once you have the two plain gloves you can begin to embellish them if you wish, or leave them plain if that is the look you desire.

Step 7: To make your gauntlets more exciting, or to tailor them to suit a particular outfit, choose trims or haberdashery you are drawn to. Choose what you would like to decorate your gauntlets with by using particular colours to theme together. You could use a certain colour palette such as blue tones, greys, metallics or natural hues to draw inspiration from. If you spot a button you are drawn to when shopping for supplies, try composing a decoration around this. For small gauntlets, less decoration is best as you don't want them to be weighed down or lose their simple silhouette. Once you have decided on the pieces you like, try the gauntlets on and balance the trims on top. When you have an arrangement you

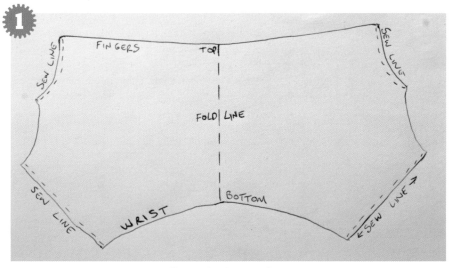

Pattern for the gauntlets.

Stitch the other side of the thumb hole and secure by tying off the thread.

Trace the pattern onto the fabric.

Stitch along the first edge.

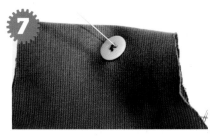

Stitch your chosen embellishment to the gauntlets.

Cut out both gauntlets and pin together, ready for sewing.

Try experimenting with different embellishments to create unique pairs of gauntlets.

are happy with, pin the trim to the glove if required and tack into place. If you have chosen buttons, stitch through the buttonholes in a cross shape to secure fully. Once you have finished adding trims, tie the thread at the end of the thread and snip off the excess.

Now you have made one pair of gauntlets, why not experiment with pairs that could be interchangeable, and try different fabrics and trims to create a pair for most outfits? Simplistic gloves work best with busier outfits and vice versa. Why not try adding ruffles to wrists, bows to thumbs and create patterns using buttons for different twists?

Customizing Goggles

Goggles are synonymous with Steampunk and, after cogs, are probably the most recognizable element in the genre. However, goggles are not the be all and end all of Steampunk and should be given a twist that makes the design original. Quite often goggles are used to make outfits look 'Steampunk' but usually these are standard off-the-shelf versions that have not been given any interesting touches. Steampunk goggles are usually decorative, not functional, as the lenses are usually similar to those used for welding and are not easy to see through. Goggles can be used as the ultimate accessory to adorn other articles of clothing such as top hats, or worn as a hairband on top of your head. For a more casual look, attach goggles to your belt so they're hanging from your hip by looping the belt through the headstrap. Wearing goggles around your neck makes an interesting alternative to a necklace and can set off a high-necked ruffle blouse.

Making goggles unique can involve many design elements and techniques, such as spray painting over the lenses, attaching chains, feathers or lace.

Experiment with your own style and add elements you find inspiring to create a singular piece to accent your outfits. Consider using paints to distress the

goggles on the frames, use lace to cover the lenses and try adding trims to the elastic strap. The more unique touches you can add, the better.

Customized goggles.

For this tutorial you will need:
1 pair of goggles
10–20 cogs and watch parts

Tools:
Strong jewellery adhesive
Pliers
Paper towels (optional)
Toothpick
Plasticine (optional)
Acrylic paints and brushes (optional)

Step 1: Prepare the goggles for decorating by giving them a gentle wipe-over with a damp cloth. This should remove any grease or residue, making the surface ready for painting and gluing. If you would like to distress the goggles with paint, do this first and leave to dry. For this project, I have chosen a pair of goggles that already have a metallic distressed paint effect; however, this is easy to replicate by using acrylic paint. To paint your goggles, cover the lenses with masking tape and mix some acrylic paint in a shade of your choice. Consider the colour of your trims and what will match. If you would like to create an opulent pair of goggles, use rich colours such as gold, burgundy and black to paint areas of the goggles and perhaps add filigree swirls and embellishments. These colours will add depth and make elements of your goggles stand out against a darker background. Should you wish to create something altogether more dystopian and post-apocalyptic, distress your goggles by stippling paint around the frames and dabbing the excess away with paper towels. This will add texture and pattern to the surface. Metallic colours are excellent for this as they will evoke thoughts of machinery and adventure, but should you wish to use matte colours these can also be just as good at creating the illusion of aged metals. Once you have painted the

Prepare your goggles ready for painting or gluing.

Begin arranging the cogs on the lenses of the goggles.

Begin gluing the cogs into place.

Layer the cogs, glue down and leave to dry.

Finished goggles.

surfaces of the goggles, leave to dry until the paint is completely dry – usually a few hours if you're using acrylic paints.

Step 2: To start work on the decoration design, gather the watch parts and cogs together. Arrange them on the parts of the goggles you would like to be decorated. You may want to consider placing cogs in consecutive connecting designs to really give a sense of functionality to them. If you would like to decorate the sides as well as the lenses of your goggles, arrange the pieces on each surface and, once you're happy with the placement, take a photograph or make a quick sketch to refer to afterwards.

Step 3: Remove all the decorative elements from the goggles and take the jewellery adhesive, toothpick and plasticine. If your goggles don't sit upright on a surface or have lenses that are too heavy, before starting to glue items on you will need to secure them to the surface you're working on so they don't fall and make the glued pieces slip or come off. Use the plasticine to stick the goggles to the work surface and check they're secure. Place your decorative elements next to your goggles so they are to hand and in gluing order. Focus on one area at a time when gluing so you don't get confused as to which element needs to be used next. If you have decided to decorate the sides of your goggles, make sure they are placed so they're flat with the side pointing upwards. Hold down using plasticine if need be; this will give you an even, level surface to work on.

Step 4: Take the jewellery adhesive and place a small dab onto the toothpick. Using your fingers or pliers, take the first element to be glued down and add

adhesive to the underside. When sufficiently covered, press down onto the goggles, using the dry end of the toothpick or the pliers. Apply even pressure so as not to lift the element away from the surface. Repeat this step for each piece until all the items have been used for that side. Leave to dry for at least two hours before moving on to the opposite side and repeating the process. Check before moving on to the opposite side that the glue has bonded with the cogs and watch parts. If some elements still feel fragile, leave to dry for another hour and test again. Should there be points that have not bonded at all, apply more glue using the toothpick. Once you have completed both sides, leave to dry for a further two hours.

Step 5: Place the goggles with the lenses facing upwards and use the plasticine to hold them upwards if required. Start gluing the back of the decorative pieces with the toothpick and adhesive and add them onto the frames around the lenses. Layer the lenses so they still look functional, leaving a small amount of the glass visible. Make the lenses individual from each other as this will make the goggles more unique. You may wish to to think about how glasses from the past looked and research functional welding goggles and optical instruments used for close-up work. You could make specific design elements by using copper wire to create shapes and gluing onto the lenses. This can be done by bending wire using pliers and wire cutters to mold into the shape you require. Once you have attached all the decorative elements and applied an even pressure to them, leave the goggles to dry for twenty-four hours before wearing. Once dry, use a paper towel to polish the lenses and remove any fingerprints or glue residue.

Epaulettes

Epaulettes usually consist of one or two decorative, ornamental shoulder pieces made as part of an item of clothing. This project will teach you how to make an epaulette that can be attached to most types of clothing or worn as a stand-alone item over a vest or similar. Epaulettes can be worn as a pair or singly. They create an exceptional silhouette and can be used to accentuate basic items in your wardrobe. You can use many things to decorate the basic epaulette shape and build upon your sewing skills.

For this tutorial you will need:
Shoulder pad
2 brooch pins
Selection of trims

Tools:
1 Sharps needle
Reels of cotton thread to match the colour of your shoulder pad and trims
Scissors

Step 1: Sketch a design for your epaulette. Take into account the shape it will have on your shoulder. You may wish to have a sharp edge to make a clear defined line on your shoulder, or it may be more your style to have a looser,

---

CUSTOMIZING EPAULETTES

I recommend sewing customized attachments onto your epaulettes to make them secure and avoid any slipping. A strong craft glue can be used to attach fabric to the basic epaulette base, but be aware that this may make your epaulettes more rigid in shape and not as malleable to your shoulder shape. Those elements not suitable for stitching to the epaulette can be glued with a hot glue gun.

Finished epaulette.

will need to be folded over the edges of the pad.

Step 3: Pin the trims into place until you're happy with the placements of each piece. Try a few different variations and don't worry if your pad ends up not resembling your previous sketch. You may find that you have to yield to the will of some trims, as they will have a natural curve or stretch that makes your design slightly different. Once you have all the elements pinned into place, try the epaulette on over your shoulder to see if any of the trims need to be moved. Consider how the epaulette looks from the front and the reverse, if any pieces are obscured by others or if some trims are not lined up correctly.

Step 4: When you're happy with your placement of the trims, begin to stitch them into place, starting from the lowest layer. Using strong stitches, add one or two stitches around the edges of the trim to hold in place. Continue to layer the trims and stitch into place, finishing with knots at the end of each line. Remove the pins as you stitch and build upon the pad, sewing all the trims into place until it is completely covered.

Step 5: Should you wish to use feather pads, be careful when stitching that you sew through the pad, avoiding the feathers, as they can begin to look sparse if they're caught inside stitches. Should you accidentally end up stitching across the feather fronds, gently pull them out of the stitches using the needle to pick them up and away from the stitch.

Step 6: Once the top trims are in place, turn the epaulette over and place the two brooch pins equidistant from one another. You will need to consider which items of clothing your epaulette will be attached to with regard to where you would like the pins to sit. For example,

ragged edge. Include other elements you would like to use, such as feathers, spikes, mechanics, faux fur, chains or any other things you can think of. Once you have created a sketch, you can then begin to plan what you would like to buy and also how you will fasten the elements to the top of your shoulder pad. Pick a colour of shoulder pad to match the trims you have chosen. Shoulder pads tend to come in a small variety of colours and most haberdashers will only stock white and black, so you may have to cover the base

pad with a fabric of your choice. This can be done by drawing around the pad onto your chosen fabric and cutting out the shape. Pin the fabric around the pad onto the underside and stitch into place using a back stitch.

Step 2: To make sure your epaulette doesn't become too heavy, choose trims that are light and not too cumbersome to decorate it. Lay out the trims and carefully measure the amounts you need to decorate the top. Allow half an inch at either end of them for the length, as they

1

Begin to design your epaulette around the shoulder pad base.

2

Measure out the trims for the epaulette.

3

Pin the trims into place.

4

Begin stitching the trims into place, starting with the lowest layer.

5

Place the feather pad on top of the epaulette and stitch into place.

6

Stitch the brooch pins into place.

with a blazer the pins will need to be at the front and back edges of the item. For a strap top, the pins would need to be at the top edge. Once you have worked out the placement for the pins, stitch them into place using the holes in the brooch pin. Pass the needle through the hole on the underside of the epaulette and loop around the end of the pin, avoid catching any of the trims above, and try to stitch the pins so the thread isn't showing on the top side of the epaulette. Repeat on the other end of the brooch,

7

Completed epaulette with feather pad.

using the opposite hole. Repeat the stitching with the second pin and fasten into place. When wearing the epaulette, be certain to make sure the safety catches on either of the pins are in place to avoid them slipping from their holder and causing injury.

Should you wish to make a matching pair of epaulettes, repeat the same steps above. Try making epaulettes that are similar but not completely matching to make them versatile as stand-alone pieces or as a statement when worn together. Should you wish to join a pair of epaulettes together, add chains and join the top corners of the pads so they reach across the top of your torso. You can pass jump rings through shoulder pads easily and these can be clamped closed using pliers. When epaulettes are joined by chains, they look great over strapless gowns and don't require pins to hold them in place. Should you require the epaulettes to sit still without moving on bare skin, use clothing or toupee tape on the back of the pad. This will secure the epaulette and keep it in place all evening.

Body Harness

A simple body harness is a good technical exercise for practising your sewing skills. A body harness can incorporate many styles and is currently seeing a revival across many styles of fashion. Harnesses can be made from a variety of fabrics depending on the style

Body harness.

you would like to replicate. Usually in Steampunk they are made of leather or thick elastic and can be designed to cross the body or be more of an open style akin to a waistcoat. Elastic is an easier fabric to work with as you will only need to measure out the elastic on your own body as opposed to making a pattern. You can purchase elastic in a limited range of colours; thicker elastics in particular tend to be easily available only in monochrome colours. This is something to bear in mind if you have a particular piece of clothing you would like to team your harness with.

There is more choice in patterns and colours with elastic webbing, but the fabric is not as stretchy as standard elastic. Some trims are made from elastic and these can be explored as an alternative material. Most elastic trims are not thick enough on their own to make a harness but could be combined with thicker elastic. Elastic is easy to embellish as it is a sturdy fabric so can be customized, but being also lightweight and stretchy you'll be able to wear it over many different outfits.

Jewellery chains can also be made into a body harness. This can be achieved by joining chain together using jump rings, mirroring the body's shape and curves. To create a delicate chain harness, use a small-link chain. Should you wish to replicate something that is more akin to body armour, use a large-link, heavy chain.

The harness shown in Fig. 149 is made from leather and backed with satin, a project for the more advanced seamstress. The harness in the tutorial is made from elastic to enable you to build your skills until you can attempt something more advanced.

For this tutorial you will need:
2–4m of thick, heavy-duty elastic
Reel of cotton thread to match the colour of your elastic
Buttons and pre-made bows

Tools:
1 Sharps needle
Scissors
Tape measure (optional)

Step 1: Begin by measuring the elastic for the waistband. Decide where you would like your waistband to sit; most harnesses sit just under the bust line. Should you wish your harness to sit lower and have longer straps, measure around your waist or hips. You can use a tape measure around your body to provide the correct measurements, but this is not really necessary as you can just use the elastic straight around your middle. Avoid stretching the elastic while doing this as you could end up with the strap being too tight. Allow an inch and a half of overlap at the ends of the elastic as this will be the point where the pieces will be stitched together. Once you have the desired length, shorten this by half an inch to make sure the harness sits snugly. Cut the elastic and pin the ends together, overlapping by an inch and a half. Set to one side.

Step 2: Measure the straps. Do this by placing the elastic strap over your shoulder until it meets the point where the waistband will sit. At this point, you can decide if you would like your straps to sit straight from shoulder to waistband, if you would like them to cross over at the neck, the back or both. Try different combinations with the loose

Measure the elastic for the waistband by measuring around your body and pin together.

Experiment with crossed over and open necklines.

elastic and see what you like best. Measure and make sure either end is even, down to the waistband point; reduce by one and a half inches to allow

Pin the shoulder straps to the inside of the waistband.

Begin to sew the shoulder straps to the waistband.

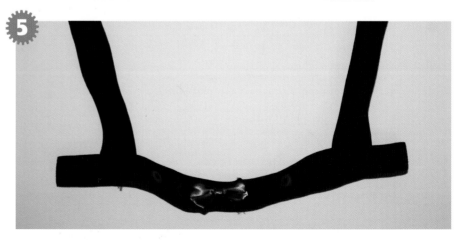

Add the embellishments onto the harness.

for the stretch of the elastic, and cut. Measure the cut strap against the remainder of elastic and cut an equal amount.

Step 3: Place the waistband down onto a flat surface, making sure the pinned area is in the middle at the back of the band. Pin the straps into place on the inside of the waistband, about two inches in from the edges, allowing them overlap on the band. This will ensure the straps have strength and are secure. Do this on the front and also the back of the waistband.

Step 4: Turn the harness inside out so the joined points of the elastic are facing outwards. Thread your needle with a double thread and tie a knot at the end. Begin to sew around the joins in a square using a running stitch and finish with a knot on each square. To make sure the elastic is incredibly secure, you may wish to sew around the square twice. Once the straps are both stitched into place on either side of the waist, at each point, make sure they're secure and add any extra stitches which may have been missed.

Step 5: Take the embellishments and place them on top of the harness in the areas you would like them. Try using bows to cover stitching or buttons to embellish the shoulder straps. Use pins to try different placements. When happy with an arrangement, sew the pieces into place one by one and finish by knotting the thread on the back of each item.

INSTANT GLAMOUR

Try sewing epaulettes onto the shoulders of a body harness. This will create an accessory that will instantly add Steampunk glamour to t-shirts, vests and blouses.

Try on the harness to check it fits correctly. If there are any problems, such as the straps being too long or too baggy, adjust and pin in before sewing into place. Check the embellishments and if you wish to add more, pin into place and repeat step five. Your harness can be worn over or under clothes, depending on the look you are trying to achieve. Should you wish to add more embellishments to your piece, try to make sure these won't conflict with outside clothing as items like cogs can get caught on fabrics.

Ray Gun

If you want to wear any of your Steampunk creations and outfits to a convention or gathering, I would encourage you to equip yourself with a fantastical ray gun. There are many ways to make ray guns, starting completely from scratch using items like washing-up liquid and plastic drinks bottles, layering paint and glue to hold them together and making something intricate and detailed. Making an item from the basics will take many hours, if not days or weeks, which is ideal if you have the time as you will have a truly unique weapon. However, there are ways to create an equally special piece by using other options such as ready-made water pistols or supersoakers and toy guns.

To create a wondrous ray gun you will need to consider how you will be using it. If you plan to wear your gun on your belt as an accessory, you will need to consider the paint you use to make sure it is non-transferable to your clothing or easily chipped. Spray paint is a recommended way of covering a gun in a quick amount of time, but you may need to apply several coats for a professional, long-lasting finish. You can layer paints to make the gun look more distressed or futuristic. One way of distressing an item is to spray paint it

Ray gun.

with a base colour, then a topcoat of a main colour, usually lighter than the base, and then lightly sand back the paint. This way you will create a two-tone layer that gives the impression of rust and weather decay.

Another way to paint your gun would be with acrylic paints, but this can be costly and time-consuming as you will need a lot of paint and a lot of time in between coats. To compromise and create something in between the two techniques, you can spray paint a base coat and use acrylic paints to add the finer details. You may wish to add elements of filigree for a Victoriana-inspired design or paint splatters for a more futuristic style, and these can only be created using brushes.

When planning your gun, sketch out your design from start to finish and have your materials ready to eliminate any mistakes that may arise from being poorly prepared. Always allow adequate drying time for your project and prepare a drying area away from any interferences such as pets or children, so that your project will not be damaged at crucial stages.

For this tutorial you will need:
Medium-sized water pistol
20–30 decorative charms, cogs and
    watch parts
Spray paint in a colour of your choice

Tools:
Glue gun
Toothpick
Pliers

Step 1: Prepare the water pistol by washing it in warm, soapy water. This will remove any residue and prepare the surface to be painted. Leave the gun to dry thoroughly or dry with a towel. Take the spray paint and protect the surrounding area with newspaper or a similar disposable material. Lay the gun down onto the surface, shake the can for one minute and begin to spray the gun at a distance of around thirty centimetres (one foot). Move the can from side to side when spraying, pausing intermittently to shake the can. Once you have a first coat on one side, leave to dry for around ten minutes until the paint is touch dry. Turn the gun over and spray on the opposite side. Leave to dry for another ten minutes and spray a second coat. Refer to the manufacturer's instructions for specific drying times for your spray paint. Once the gun is sufficiently covered, leave to dry for twenty-four hours before moving on to the next step.

Step 2: Plug in the glue gun to heat up

Prepare the gun for spraying and apply the paint.

Start adhering the decorations onto your gun.

Experiment with placements of your chosen decorations.

Try attaching an unusual material to your ray gun such as tubular crinoline.

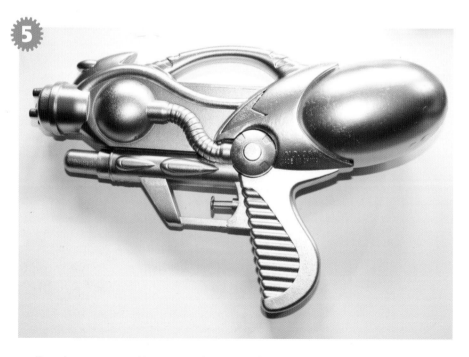

Turn the gun over and begin to replicate your design on the opposite side to finish.

while you prepare the next step. Pick out charms, watch parts, mechanics and any other decorations you would like to use on your gun. You may wish to do some research online to see how others have made their ray guns. There is a wealth of inspiration out there to guide you on the best elements to choose and on what will work best for the particular look you're going for. Once you have selected the elements you would like to use, start to place them onto the gun in an arrangement. You will need to yield to the curves and structure of the gun when placing your arrangement, as some items will not stick to curved edges or may overlap areas like the trigger or handle. Try several different placements and take photos or make a sketch of each one before you settle on a final choice for the design.

Step 3: Once you have a placement in mind that you would like to use, lay out the pieces you need to glue onto the gun in order. Position the gun flat on a steady surface, and work from the back of the gun to the tip. This will prevent you from knocking glued items with your hand while you're working along the gun. Take the glue gun and a toothpick and add a small dab of glue to the end. Use a toothpick to transfer the glue to each component while holding it with pliers to make the application more precise. However, if you're confident enough with the glue gun, you can apply glue directly to the gun and press the components down into it. When a sufficient amount of adhesive has been placed on the item, press it down onto the gun using an even pressure. Repeat with each piece until one side is decorated. Leave the piece to dry for twenty-four hours before turning over to decorate the opposite side. This will stop any of the components dropping off or the glue adhering to a surface.

Step 4: To add an extra element of design to your gun, it is possible to use futuristic-looking materials to create a different look. For the modern sci-fi look in this tutorial, I used a small section of tubular crinoline – a material usually reserved for making lightweight hair pieces and millinery – to the end of the ray gun. The crinoline I have used is woven with metallic gold so it creates an electric-type look. To attach the piece of crinoline, simply add a dab of glue at each end and hold down into place for a few minutes until dry. Experiment with different materials – this will give you a better understanding of what will and won't work.

Step 5: For the opposite side, you can repeat step 3 if you would like the gun to be exactly the same. Or to create something different on each side, refer to the sketches or photographs you made previously and choose a design from there. Again, glue the items down using the tips in step 3. Leave to dry for at least twenty-four hours before use to give the glue time to set.

Ray Gun Holster Belt

In order to be able to wear a ray gun as part of your outfit, you will need a way to attach it to you. When making an item that is meant to be decorative yet potentially functional, you will need to consider a few design essentials: the belt will need to be able to support the weight of the gun, the gun will need to be secure yet accessible as you will more than likely want to show off your handiwork to others, and the gun needs to remain protected to avoid any accidental damage.

To make a base for your belt you will need a substantial weighted material such as leather. It is advisable to buy a ready-made belt and add to this, as it will be more cost- and time-effective. To ensure you have considered all the design specifications you will need for your belt, take your gun and hold it in the position where you would like to hang on your body or sit on the belt base. You can then start to sketch out a design based on this placement. You want to avoid anything heavy over sensitive areas of the body, and be aware that the gun may be uncomfortable rubbing against bare skin if you plan to wear it with a crop top or similar. By making detachable straps for your holster to hang from, you can make holsters interchangeable without having to waste more material on new attachments every time. Should you wish to make the holster all in one piece that will also loop around the belt, you can cut the straps into the original triangle piece.

For this tutorial you will need:
1 plain or patterned belt, preferably leather
1 leather off-cut, around 50cm wide
10–15 metal eyelets
50cm chain or ribbon
1m thin ribbon in a colour of your choice

Tools:
Scissors or rotary cutter and cutting mat
Pen
Eyelet tool
Round- and flat-nosed pliers
Leather or strong craft glue

Step 1: Place the gun on top of the leather. Roughly draw a triangle shape pointing downwards from the handle to the tip of the gun. Leaving a two-inch allowance for the seam, trace around the gun, bringing the edges of the leather together to make sure the gun will fit inside the holster. If you're not very comfortable with drawing a straight line

Ray gun holster.

Step 3: When you have cut out the piece of leather, you will need to prepare it to be stuck together. Fold in half and check that the edges meet with no overhang from either side. If the edges overhang, use the scissors or rotary cutter to trim off the excess until they meet correctly. Open out the leather, take the leather glue and begin to place a thin line amount onto the inside rough edge of the material, about half an inch in from the very edge. Stop when you reach about three-quarters of the way up as this is the place that will be laced together with eyelets so it won't need to be glued. Use another small piece of leather, old store card or plastic glue stick to spread the glue evenly towards the edges, but avoid spreading right to the very edge. Follow the manufacturer's instructions as to when to join the two edges together. Some glues should be joined instantly for a good strong bond, but others will need time to dry to a tacky state before being stuck together.

Fold the leather over so the shiny side is facing upwards and press together by pinching all the way along the edge. If any glue should escape through the join, use the leather scrap, card or glue stick to remove the excess. If you spill any glue onto the smooth side of the leather, be sure to remove it straight away as craft glue can stain darker leathers. Leave the glue to dry overnight and check the next day that it has adhered correctly. If there are any areas which aren't sticking, add a touch more glue and leave again to dry overnight.

Step 4: When the holster is dry, it is time to put the eyelets in place. Take the eyelet tool and use it to punch through the leather on the upper quarter of the holster. Make holes on either side of the leather that are level with each other. To do this take the two pieces of leather on the top quarter of the holster and use the tool to squeeze an indent on either side

freehand, use a ruler to mark out the lines.

Step 2: Once you are happy with the shape of the holster and have checked

that the seams will meet with enough space for the gun, begin to cut the leather with a pair of scissors or a rotary cutter (if using a rotary cutter, make sure you do this on top of a protective cutting mat).

while the holster is flat. Be careful to make the indents at least half a centimetre away from the edge so the eyelet has enough material to surround it.

Step 5: Use the indents as a guide for the eyelet placements. Place the eyelet down onto the marked indent with the flared opening facing upwards. Use the eyelet tool to press either side of one piece of leather. This will force the eyelet through the leather and flare the back out, holding it in place. Should you have any trouble in passing the eyelet through the leather, use round-nosed pliers to widen the hole slightly by pushing one side through a millimetre at a time. Be careful not to widen the hole too much as this will cause the eyelet to fall out. Make sure the eyelet tool is the correct way round when punching the eyelet through as otherwise the eyelet will remain intact and not flare as it should. The extended pin of the tool should point downwards through the flared hole and the flat circle of the hole should be underneath the straight part of the eyelet. Once you have added one eyelet, work alternating from side to side until the required number of eyelets are in place. Check all the eyelets on the reverse to make sure they have flared over the surrounding leather and that they are secure. If any eyelets aren't secure, use pliers to peel the flared edges upwards and remove and replace with a new eyelet.

Step 6: Once the eyelets are in place, take the ribbon and use it to lace the holster together, threading from the top towards the bottom. If you're unsure how to lace the holster, think of how you would lace shoes and try that technique. Making the ribbon even on both sides is fairly aesthetically important, so you will need to experiment as to which lacing techniques work best. Try passing the ribbon over the top of the eyelets for

more decorative lacing, or under the eyelets for a functional look; it comes down to personal preference. You could experiment with contrasting colours, two or more ribbons, shoe laces, chain – you really can use whatever you would like to here. To hold your lacing in place, use a bow to tie ribbon and shoelaces, and jump rings to join chains together.

Step 7: To attach your holster to your belt, you need some belt clips. These can be made by creating two strips of leather that contain eyelets and by hanging them onto your belt using chain or ribbon. To create the loops, measure the width of your belt on one side and add an extra inch onto your measurement. Double the measurement to account for the other side of your belt and make a strip two inches wide plus the length of your measurement. When you have sketched out the strip, repeat the same sized strip for the second loop. Cut both strips out of the leather using a rotary cutter or scissors.

Step 8: Grab the eyelet tool and use it to mark the indent for your eyelets like you did in step 5. Punch one eyelet through the bottom of each end of the strips and insert an eyelet into each of the four holes. Check the eyelets have flared out correctly and are in place and secure.

Step 9: Try the belt on and work out where you would like the holster to sit. Place the strips of the loops onto the belt so they are sitting next to each other. Measure the gap between the top of the holster and the eyelet of each loop on the belt. Take the measurement and transfer it to the chain or ribbon you would like to use to attach the holster. Once measured, double the length of your chosen material and set to one side.

Step 10: Before being able to join the holster to the belt loops, you will need to

add two eyelets to the top of the holster on each side at the edge of the straps. Work out the spots you would like to put the eyelets through by positioning the holster at the angle you would like it and pinching the areas between your thumb and forefinger. This should give you a rough idea of how the angle will transpose once they're joined with chain or ribbon. When you're happy with the angle of the holster, make an indent on the leather at the four points using the eyelet tool. Once you have indented the leather, use the eyelet tool to place the eyelets through both sides of the holster. Check the eyelets are fully inserted into the leather with the backs flared out.

Step 11: Take the chain or ribbon that was measured out earlier and lie it out flat. Thread one piece of the chain or ribbon through the left-hand leather strip through both eyelets. Bring the chain down to the eyelets on the top of the holster on the left-hand side and loop until both ends meet. Open a jump ring with a pair of round-nosed pliers and attach both ends of the chain to either side of the ring. Close the jump ring and repeat for the other side until the holster hangs from the belt. If you have decided to use ribbon to join the holster, thread the ribbon through the top eyelet and down to the eyelet on the holster. Pull the ribbon through and tie together in a loop and repeat for the other side. Alternatively, you could use one length of ribbon and thread it through the top eyelet, down to the holster, thread through the back eyelet, through the front and up to the empty top eyelet through to the back, down to the bottom holster eyelet, back over the front to make an 'X' shape and back through the eyelet you started with. Tie off at the back to secure in place.

Step 12: Once you have finished your holster and belt, you can decorate them

Draw around the ray gun in a triangle shape, leaving a two-inch seam allowance.

Insert the eyelets into the leather.

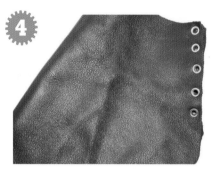

Mark the place for your eyelets on both sides.

Cut the leather, making sure the seams meet.

Lace the holder together using ribbon.

Place the leather strips over the belt and measure the ribbon to thread them on with, and cut.

Attach the two edges together using the leather glue.

Cut out two strips of leather to create the belt straps.

Add four eyelets to the top of the holster, on each side.

10

Thread the ribbon through the holster and loops to bring together.

11

Try different decorations on your ray gun belt and different styles of holster.

in any style you wish. Why not use some of your new-found techniques to customize the piece in a style that is all your own? You could try sewing items to the holster, using leather appliqués to cut out and stick on, attach more chains, even try making small leather pockets to make the belt into more of a utility style. The possibilities are truly endless and should help to inspire you with further design choices. Having said that, a plain holster in a luxurious colour can also make a strong, simple statement on its own.

Chapter 8
The Captain of the Airship

fiction is to the grown man what play is to the child; it is there that he changes the atmosphere and tenor of his life.
– ROBERT LOUIS STEVENSON

Men's Steampunk Projects

Modern men's fashion, apart from a few exceptions, tends to be fairly formulaic and repetitive from season to season. Often I find that men are delighted when they discover that I offer a bespoke men's range of jewellery as it can be difficult to acquire unique items on the high street, particularly anything Steampunk-related. In men's Steampunk fashion, it is a good design choice to play with the different sub-genres to avoid an outfit looking like fancy dress or cosplay. To pair many similar items with one theme could result in an outfit looking over-styled. I would advise you to concentrate on making your individual projects distinctive from each other.

Mix up colours to add an extra element of depth, try contrasting materials and keep accessories minimal. Use a colour palette to group your ideas when designing. There are a few rules of thumb that should be followed: most colours are fine to wear together but accessories should be kept to similar tones. It is considered careless to wear a black belt with brown shoes and vice versa as it lacks attention to detail. Shirts should always be teamed with an appropriate outer layer like a waistcoat or suit jacket to give the air of sophistication that

Steampunk requires. To make sure you're teaming the correct colours, search online to find a colour wheel. There are plenty of explanations on how to use this online and it is a great way of finalizing those agonizing decisions and eliminating the guesswork out of combining colours. Pin one to your wardrobe door or mirror to remind yourself what matches as you dress.

When planning an outfit, borrow elements from things that are inspiring to you. These inspirations need not be Steampunk-related at all; in fact it's best to combine ideas from outside the Steampunk genre to help create a novel composition that will be unique to your personal style.

Teaming items from different periods of fashion is another way of harnessing your look – perhaps you prefer '60s sci fi, or Edwardian finery? Whatever you are influenced by should be reflected in your designs and also your outfits. Often, finding one or two items of clothing that will be your staple pieces will help you to build upon your wardrobe. Try searching flea markets, vintage shops, eBay and other places which may have retro clothing and you're bound to find pieces that no one else has. Try to pick pieces

that will be versatile within your wardrobe and that you can dress up or down, as you can always add minimal accessories to an outfit to enhance it. If you develop and create your own version of Steampunk style, it will be easy to define what will suit you and what won't, which will make it easier in the future to design appropriately themed items.

Tutorial 1: Leather Cuffs

Cuffs can add an air of masculinity to more effeminate outfits as they add a hard line to potentially soft materials such as silks and chiffons or velvet.

Leather cuff.

When considering how you would like to make your cuff, take into account the amount of time you have available and decide if you want to start completely from scratch by making a pattern and purchasing leather to make the piece in its entirety. Consider the types of fastenings you would like to use and also if these would be compatible for a handmade piece or a customized pre-made strap. The most simple fastenings can provide a delicate finish, such as lacing your cuff together or by using a pre-made watch strap to create the joins.

To give your cuff a streamlined look you could use popper fastenings, but these require specific tools to secure them into the material, which can be costly if you are only going to make one or two cuffs. However, if you find cuffs to be an accessory you gel with and enjoy making, then it would be cost-effective to purchase the equipment to put these in place. A good quality basic leatherwork tool kit can be a good investment if the material becomes something you would like to progress with and develop in other projects. It will save time in the long run and give a more professional finish to any pieces you decide to make with the kit.

For this project I have chosen an inexpensive leather punch eyelet tool as this gives a professional-looking finish to a project. This particular tool can be used for other crafts and projects as it will, with some simple manipulation, create holes in paper and other fabrics which makes it a sensible investment. To get yourself acquainted with the leather tool and to ease you into working with a potentially stubborn material, try buying a pre-made leather watch strap and customize this. Then you could move on to trying to cut your own patterns for cuffs. These can be made by cutting strips of leather that are the same circumference measurement as your wrist and adding eyelets along the two

adjoining edges. The eyelets can then be laced together to create a cuff.

For this tutorial you will need:
Pre-made leather watch band
6 (or more) 5mm jump rings
6 (or more) eyelets
6 (or more) metal charms of your
    choice

Tools:
Leather eyelet tool
Flat-nosed pliers
Round-nosed pliers
Chalk

Step 1: Set out the leather band, eyelets, charms and jump rings. Begin by opening the jump rings so they are ready for later on. Lay out the watch strap and work out where you would like the charms to hang. The charms should be located one centimetre apart from each other to allow for the spacing of the eyelets and about half a centimetre in from the edge of the band, avoiding any stitching, bands or connector holes. Measure the spacing in between where you would like the eyelets to be and mark the back of the band with a piece of chalk. Using the width of an eyelet in between each hole will make them fairly spaced and not too crowded. Use the eyelet tool to mark the leather along the band by putting it either side of the band and squeezing together. Check all the marked holes are in the correct place and adjust if needs be.

Step 2: When you're ready, use the eyelet tool to push the metal through the leather. The eyelet should go easily into the leather, but if there are any issues you may need to make a small hole. This can be done by passing one side of a pair of round-nosed pliers into the hole, which will help to expand it and make it easier to pass the eyelet into. Once the eyelet is in the hole, press down on the

Set out tools and equipment.

Mark the eyelet holes along the strap using the eyelet tool.

eyelet using the pointed part of the tool and allow the back of the eyelet to flare over the back of the band.

Step 3: Gather together the charms you have chosen. The charms used in this piece are following an adventurer theme. You may wish to think about a theme for your cuff or you could just pick pieces you are drawn to. Whatever collection of pieces you decide upon, make sure the

Press the eyelets into the band.

Place the charms onto the open jump rings.

Close the jump rings on the charms.

tones are matching or fairly similar. Using gold and silver together is an option but it may muddle the design of your piece and not provide a clear definitive stamp to your cuff. Place each charm onto one of the open jump rings that were set aside earlier.

Step 4: Place each jump ring in turn through an eyelet and close off using the pliers. Once all the jump rings are closed together, your piece is ready to wear. Now that you have practised with this style of cuff, try making your own from scratch or using other design ideas. Leather is great for cuffs but is not the be all and end all of cuff materials. You may want to try using more industrial-type materials for more of a post-apocalyptic look, or soft materials for a look inspired by Victorian gents. You could even try combining some elements from a few sub-genres to inspire you into creating cuffs that enhance a number of outfits. Whatever look you decide to go for, be creative with the design stage and use the planning stage for encouragement. If you end up with several designs, don't feel you have to make every single version of the cuffs; pick your favourite and work from that one. You can always use the other designs later on.

Once the cuff is finished, you can replicate the design on another pre-made band using the same or different charms. Try layering cuffs to achieve a stronger style and more of a statement look to wrists. This look is great paired with a shirt with rolled up sleeves and a jabot.

Tutorial 2: Top Hat Band

A top hat can be a valuable staple item in your Steampunk wardrobe and provides a good basis for most outfits. To make your top hat versatile and prevent it from becoming a stale style choice, you can create interchangeable top hat bands. These can be made from all manner of materials, can be simple or intricate, and can contain any elements of design that you find inspiring. Another way to decorate your hat is to add silk or chiffon scarves around the base or mid section; these can be teamed with an elasticated top hat band to create density and bulk to the accessory. For everyday wear, you can use your band to harmonize with your outfit choices. Choose a few different colours for your bands and make sure that they match the base colour of your hat. If your hat is black, you can blend most colours with this; if you have chosen another colour such as brown, purple or perhaps burgundy, stick to softer colours with a chalky or cream undertone such as slate grey, pale green or dusky blue. Should you wish to use a contrasting colour for your band, be sure to create a strong contrast as anything else may look as if you haven't thought about the choice.

You can embellish your band with any items you are drawn to: gems, feathers, cogs, maybe a few shells or even folded pages from books will all make pleasant additions. Try first to make a plain band and then add decorations to it. You'll need to bear in mind how you will attach your embellishments to your band and how this will affect their placement on your hat. To make this project quick and easier to make you can use a hot glue gun or a heavy duty craft glue. If you want your project to last indefinitely you should sew the embellishments to your band to make them stand the test of time. However, hot glue and strong craft glue will hold things in place for quite some time if you look after the band and make sure it is stored safely when not worn.

For this tutorial you will need:
1 elasticated headband in a similar colour to your top hat
1 offcut of felt in a similar colour to your top hat
1–3 small to medium decorations such as watch face, cameo, key or cogs
25cm lace in a colour of your choice
25cm ribbon in a colour of your choice
3–5 feathers, medium length
1 artificial flower

Tools:
Glue gun
Scissors
Iron (optional)

Step 1: Before you begin making your top hat band, it is a good idea to sketch out what you would like it to look like. If you have no ideas in mind, try and take inspiration by telling a story with your band. For example, if you had a celebrity in mind and they commissioned you to create a top hat band, what would you design for them? Sketch your designs out and don't be afraid to go a little over the top as you can always strip the ideas back and pare them down for the final piece. Once you have a sketch you would like to create, you can build upon the following steps or tailor them to your own needs. Choose the materials you would like to use and, with weight in mind, try to make your choices light. The elastic headband will not support heavy items and could end up leaning over, not sitting right and causing the top hat to tilt. When you have gathered your materials, switch on the glue gun and allow it to heat up.

Step 2: Lay the elasticated headband on a flat surface with the metal connector clamp at the back. Take the felt and, using the edge of the band as a guide, cut out a square approximately two inches squared. The felt will provide the basis for the materials to be adhered to, making the pieces secure on their own stand-alone island. If the band was used as the point to attach materials to alone, it would stretch out and cause the adhered items to fall off. Depending on how grandiose you would like your band to be, you may need to increase the size of the felt square. If you're uncertain whether two inches squared will be a large enough size for your materials, try laying out all the items to be included on your band in a rough order on the felt offcut. This will give you an idea of the space you require for the felt and avoid wasting the offcut unnecessarily. Once the square has been cut out, place the square under the side of your band. Use the heated glue gun to place a thin strip of glue along the width of the felt, half an inch up from the bottom edge. Fold the bottom edge of felt around the band so it connects with the back of the square and the glue. Press down, avoiding getting any hot glue on your skin, and hold in place for a few minutes until the temperature starts to drop or the glue starts to harden.

Top hat band.

Step 3: Gather the other materials together and start to arrange in your chosen design. Start to prepare your pieces in order, starting with the items that will be at the back of your ensemble. It is best to place larger, longer items at the back and smaller pieces towards the front or else they may become lost. Add a small amount of glue on the felt square and begin to add the longest feathers first. If your feathers have a natural curve towards the top, don't be afraid to have them going in different directions from each other. Try and place the feather shafts as close as possible together as these will need to be wrapped after gluing to cover the felt. Glue the feathers in place in turn and layer them to create an interesting pattern. Try adding a feature feather to the centre of the bunch; use a bright unnatural colour that mirrors the colour of your ribbon, or a stunning organic item like a peacock feather. Once all the feathers are glued in place, leave to dry for a few minutes so the glue begins to harden.

Step 4: Unravel the ribbon that will bind your feather shafts. If the ribbon is creased it will need to be ironed as it is being glued in a way that could exacerbate any wrinkles. When ironing ribbon, use an iron on a low heat and cover with a tea towel to avoid it melting. After ironing, leave the ribbon to cool completely. Test the wrapping style around the base of your feathers before you glue in place. Be sure to use the ribbon to also cover the back of the felt on the section which holds the feathers. Overlap the ribbon where possible as this will produce a nice texture to the piece and avoid any unsightly gaps which may form, revealing the glue underneath. When you're happy with the wrapping, remove the ribbon and add glue along a section at a time,

starting from the end. Begin to wrap the feathers slowly and press down evenly to adhere the glue to the surface. Keep the ribbon taught and even while wrapping so the sections don't ruche by mistake. When you have sufficiently wrapped the shafts, cut the ribbon and add glue to the end to stop it from fraying. Make sure the end is tucked behind the feathers and out of sight. If you would like to make a design feature out of the end of the ribbon, cut an upside down 'V' shape into the last centimetre and glue in place. Leave the glue for a few minutes to set.

Step 5: Using a larger piece of decoration such as an artificial flower, prepare the back by making sure it is textured enough to hold the glue and the felt surface together. Position in an area that is not the centre and not too focal as you want this element to provide bulk to the design and an aesthetic presence, but not to overpower the piece. Try a few placements before deciding on where you would like it to sit permanently. When you are happy with the placement, add a medium to large dab of glue to the reverse of the flower and press down evenly, but not too forcefully, for three to five minutes until the glue has begun to harden. Leave for a further five minutes to dry before moving on to the next step so as not to disturb the flower. Should the flower not adhere correctly first time, remove from the square and use a larger dab of glue. Some types of artificial flower are not compatible with hot glue and will simply not adhere due to the texture of the surface. If this is the case with your flower, stitch a small piece of felt to the reverse as this will act as a good bonding point for the hot glue.

Step 6: Applying the lace can be tricky as it requires a certain amount of manipulation to keep the glue from

escaping through the holes and stopping it from adhering securely. To cover the fact that lace can sometimes look rather tatty when glued with hot glue, you will need to hide the top of the application site. The large flower will be the perfect distraction from this and provide an overlap which should disguise any potential messiness. Fold the lace over in half in the centre but make the ends flare out in a ' < ' shape. Add a thin strip of glue to the reverse at the fold point. Position the lace so it is disguised by one of the petals on the flower and press down. Be careful here as the glue will most likely seep through the lace. Protect your finger by holding the lace down through the petal. Hold for two to three minutes until you can feel the glue starting to cool and set.

Step 7: Gather the larger pieces of decoration that you set aside earlier and place them in the order you would like to use them. For some pieces which may be slightly heavier (keys for example), use ribbon to hold them in place and glue to the felt or bound feathers. Use a small strip of ribbon, slightly wider than the decorative item, and add glue to the top and bottom edges on one side. Place the decoration in your desired spot and press the ribbon down on the bottom side first and then the top side. This should hold the piece in place. Should you require more stability, add glue to all four sides of the ribbon and then press down. This will ensure your piece is very firmly in place.

Step 8: Take the other two pieces of decoration and, building on the band, adjust their placement to suit. Add glue to the back of one piece and again, press down firmly yet evenly onto the felt until the glue begins to harden. Repeat for the other decorative item. Assess the band to check that all the felt has been covered or the amount left showing is minimal. If

1

Choose the band you would like to use.

2

Cut out a felt square and glue to the band.

3

Add feathers to the felt square.

4

Wrap the feather shafts in ribbon and glue into place.

5

Glue the artificial flower to the band.

6

Cut the lace and fold, then glue to the band.

7

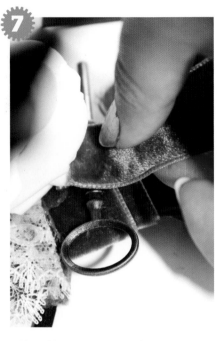

Use ribbon to secure any larger pieces.

8

Build up the decoration on the band and glue into place.

there are noticeable gaps, use more decorations to cover these. Items like buttons will also work as a great and easy way to fill medium- to large-sized spaces.

Step 9: When you're happy with your band, leave to dry for a few hours until the glue has become reasonably set. When the band feels secure and dry, place around your top hat to check the placement of the decorations. If you're happy with the design, leave the band to dry around the top hat so everything dries solidly in an upright position. If any of the glue is still tacky by this point (if using hot glue it should be dry fairly quickly), place a piece of baking or wax paper behind the band to avoid damaging the top hat. Should you be unhappy with any placements on the band after trying it on, you can try to gently remove the incorrect pieces and glue them down again.

Try making several different bands using different materials – an easy and cheap way to update a top hat and keep it looking fresh. You can also use the customized goggles as a top hat band as they add an adventurous touch.

Tutorial 3: Long Cog Chain

Steampunk jewellery for gentlemen can vary from piece to piece but usually tends to be heavy and substantial, which may not be a look you wish to emulate. To create something more delicate, you can take some of the key essentials from Steampunk like cogs and turn them into a piece that can be worn with virtually anything. A long chain can be worn in a few ways: hanging long, tucked into a waistcoat pocket, wrapped round your wrist or wrapped once around the neck to layer the chain. You can add as many cogs as you would like to your chain or leave it fairly sparse if that's what you prefer. It is important to incorporate your personal preference into your design as it will make your item more unique to your individual sense of style. If you are not partial to a necklace, you could turn your piece into a pocket watch chain by adding a safety pin at either end in a colour to match.

For this tutorial you will need:
24in chain in a colour of your choice
15 cogs
5mm jump ring
3mm jump ring
1 lobster clasp

Tools:
Pliers

Step 1: Measure out twenty-four inches of chain onto a flat surface using a tape measure. If you want your chain to be shorter, you could try an eighteen- or twenty-inch chain. This will sit higher up on the chest. Try out different lengths without cutting the chain and when you are happy with the length, mark with a small piece of sticky or masking tape. Separate the chain by using the pliers to open the adjoining links. Stretch the chain out so you are able to select the last link at the end.

Long cog chain.

Step 2 : Add the lobster clasp to one end of the chain using a jump ring. Open the jump ring and thread through the end of the chain and close together with the pliers. Avoid adding the jump ring to the other end of the chain just yet as you will need the end free to thread the cogs onto. The jump ring can be added at the end of the project.

Step 3: Take around fifteen cogs with open centres or holes big enough to pass the chain through. Begin to slide the cogs onto the chain one by one in a pattern you are happy with. You can loop the cogs onto the chain by using one of the openings on the cog, or you could weave them onto the chain by going in one side and out the other. Either style will work and both are good ways of displaying the cogs. Weaving the cogs onto the chain will make them quite prevalent and more obvious, whereas sliding the cogs on with the one loop will make them more concealed and less of a statement, while still adding a touch of Steampunk. Once the cogs have started to collect at the centre point and the chain looks like it is beginning to get crowded, start to space the cogs out by pulling them up a few links at a time. Check to see how the chain will look on by holding it up to your neck. If the chain looks sparse, add some more cogs until you feel the piece looks full. The cogs will naturally congregate at the centre point of the chain when wearing, so from time to time you can spread them out if you wish.

Step 4: If you want your cogs to hang independently and not bunch together, you can add them to the chain using small 3mm individual jump rings. In this way the cogs will stop moving along the links and each of them will stay in its individual spot. This will make them really focal and obvious, if that is the look you want to achieve. Once the cogs are in your preferred placement, finish the chain by adding the 5mm jump ring to the end and join together with a lobster clasp.

To protect the chain when you're not wearing it, keep it out of sunlight and away from other metals. This will prevent any unnecessary wear to the chain and prevent any discoloration of the metal. Try wearing the chain against a simple plain t-shirt or a white casual shirt. It will make the chain stand out from the plain background, adding finesse to any outfit.

Measure out the chain for your necklace.

Add the clasp to the end of the chain.

Thread the cogs onto the chain.

Add the jump ring to the end of the chain and spread out the cogs until you're happy with their placement.

Tutorial 4: Cravat Pin

A cravat is a versatile accessory that can be bought or made to your own specifications. Cravats add an instant piece of history to an outfit as they were the forerunner of the tailored tie that we know today. A cravat can be made out of most materials, but it is best to use something that will stay plumped up when wearing so as to create the illusion of a full neckline between a shirt and a waistcoat. Cravats are ideal if you're uncomfortable wearing a shirt fully buttoned up to the neck as they provide a space blocker, which means you won't have to show any skin. Cravats have seen a revival amongst celebrities in the last few years, with materials like silks and chiffons being turned into sophisticated pieces.

A humble cravat pin provides a focal point to your chosen material. To avoid any incidents with uncapped sharp pins, it is advised to use a larger brooch pin to decorate your cravat. This means you can use your cravat pin on a number of items, from suit jackets, top hat bands or even attached to your waistcoat. The cravat pin can also be teamed with the jabot project. Try making both of these projects with a theme in mind to allow you to seamlessly join them with other outfits.

For this tutorial you will need:
Decorative brooch pin with a flat base
Large key
Fabric flower
Cameo mounted on a plastic base, or
　　wooden cameo
25cm lace
Decorations such as artificial leaves or
　　feathers

Tools:
Hot glue gun
Scissors

Cravat pin.

Step 1: Start by taking the brooch pin and checking the area you will be adhering the items to. If the base is textured you can move on to step 2. If the base is smooth, you may need to add some texture for the glue to be able to adhere correctly. Use a small piece of sandpaper to sand in one direction at a time. Check between each buff that the texture is forming and when a light texture has developed, this will be enough to adhere the glue to. If the surface is becoming smoother with each buff, try sanding back across the texture to lift some of the surface.

Give the surface a wipe down with a damp cloth to remove the dust, and dry completely before using. Gather the other materials together and try a few different placements to see what works. A good tip is to use larger decorations towards the back and smaller decorations towards the front. The cravat pin should emulate a flower arrangement such as a corsage and be a focal point to enhance the item of clothing you are wearing it on. Don't be afraid to take inspiration from floral displays for this project. Many traditional cravat pins, which are usually just one jewel on a long pin, have floral motifs, feature cameos or take inspiration from more obviously feminine design elements. Playing up the Steampunk style by making the cravat pin larger and more flamboyant will add a touch of theatrical drama to the piece. Sketch the different placements and decide which one you would like to use.

Step 2: Place the brooch pin on a flat surface. If needs be, secure the pin with a piece of sticky tack or plasticine to keep it upright and sturdy while you apply the adhesive. The brooch pin needs to remain flat on the surface to give the hot glue a chance to dry, and to stop the glued pieces slipping. Take the

first item to be stuck to the brooch; in this case I've chosen plastic leaves. Test the placement and check that the angle of the adornment is aligned correctly, pointing outwards and away from the centre of the body. Add a dab of hot glue onto the base and press the piece into it. Hold the adornment still until the glue begins to harden or becomes opaque in colour.

Step 3: Leave the glue to dry for a few minutes; while you're waiting, you can prepare the lace. Fold the lace in half into a sideways '<' shape. You can either stitch the lace into this shape using a tacking stitch or glue into place using seam glue or a tiny dab of hot glue. If using seam glue, leave the lace to dry for thirty to sixty minutes until it has begun to harden. If using hot glue on the lace, wait until the glue has begun to turn opaque or hardens. Be aware when using glue on lace that you may encounter some bleed-through on the fabric. Don't be too concerned about being neat with the lace join as this will be covered by other components. Use a small amount of glue and superficially bond the piece, as the joined area will be covered later by the larger decorations and won't be seen.

When the lace is prepared, work out the best placement on your piece for it. Usually placing the lace at a downwards angle will make it hang correctly and sit well. However, try different positions until you're happy with how it looks. Be aware that the placement you choose may allow the lace to interact more with the main body of the brooch and be more focal to the piece. When you're happy with the placement, use hot glue to secure it into place by adding a thin line to the back of the fold and pressing onto the brooch base or leaves that are already in place. Leave to dry for a few minutes to allow the glue time to harden, then move on to the next step.

Step 4: For this next step, you will need to either create a fabric flower or use a pre-made one bought from a haberdasher's. If you're short on time and able to easily purchase a fabric flower, I would recommend doing this. However, if you have a specific colour scheme in mind or would like to give your brooch that extra handmade touch, you can create a flower from fabric. There are many different techniques and tutorials on how to do this and you will find a wealth of information online. To create a fabric flower of your own, you can follow the leather flower necklace tutorial that was featured earlier in the book but substitute the material for something less firm. A leather flower would also work in this instance and might be a subtle way to co-ordinate a couples outfit.

Place the flower in a central position on the brooch and check that the flower has enough surface area to adhere to. The area to adhere to must be secure on the reverse and be attached to the base of the pin. If the flower is attached to an area that isn't adhered to the pin then the weight of the flower will cause the leaves to fall forward. When you have checked the area, add a medium to large amount of glue to the back of the flower and press down. Depending on the type of material your flower is made from, you may need to be careful that the glue doesn't seep through. This is more likely to happen if you're using a porous material such as cotton or lace. Hold the flower in place for a few minutes until the glue has started to dry. If you're not keen on using a floral motif, you could replace this with feathers placed in a pattern to create wings on either side of the pin, or another larger decorative frame for the cameo. You could even scour charity shops and car boot sales for smaller decorative frames to house the centre cameo. Larger frames can be added to the piece by using hot glue

① Try different placements of the component parts until you're happy with the design.

② Glue the first component part onto the brooch back.

③ Prepare the lace and adhere to the first component part.

④ Add the artificial flower to the brooch.

⑤ Add the cameo to the centre of the flower and glue in place.

⑥ Add a key to the brooch pin bar to complete the piece.

and leaving to dry until adhered strongly.

Step 5: To finish the centre of the brooch, take the centrepiece you wish to use, such as a cameo. Prepare the cameo, if you're using a frame around the cabochon, and glue with a strong jewellery adhesive. Ideally this should be done twenty-four hours beforehand so the jewellery glue has a chance to dry fully. If using a wooden cameo without a frame, you can glue the cameo straight onto the centre of the flower. Try different placements around the brooch for the cameo so you can see which is the most appealing. If you have gone for a more off-centre brooch, it may be best to also place the cameo somewhere that's not central. However, if you have been leaning towards a symmetrical piece, it is better to stick with this theme to avoid the brooch looking like you may have made a mistake.

When you're happy with how the cameo looks on the pin, you can start to glue it into place. Try using an amount of glue that feels suitable for the weight of the adornment you have chosen. If you're using a metal frame on the pin, add a medium to large amount of glue. If you're using a lighter wooden cameo, a small to medium dab of glue should be enough to hold the piece in place. Leave to dry for a few minutes and check that the cameo feels like it is adhering to the base well. If you're in doubt and the cameo feels insecure, add another dab of glue to the back of the piece. This may require you to remove the cameo from the flower. Be careful when doing this as you may dislodge the other items glued onto the pin. Remove the cameo slowly and carefully with one hand while holding the flower down with the other hand. Once you feel the cameo begin to lift, you should be able to place the nozzle of the glue gun into the gap and squeeze another small amount of glue in. When the cameo feels secure, leave the whole piece to dry for at least an hour before wearing.

Step 6: To finish the pin, if the brooch back has a wide arm pin, add a hanging charm such as a key, large cog or even a skull. This adds movement to the piece when worn and makes it more eye-catching. You could also try hanging another charm from the holes on the pin. Some pins will have more holes along them than others so will facilitate more pieces. To attach the charms, use a large enough jump ring to allow movement of the item and slot through the hole, closing with pliers. If you decide to add more charms, check that they will hang below the larger adornments on the pin, such as the lace and leaves, or else they will be obscured from view. You could

even use chain to hang from the pin, which you could attach to a pocket watch.

Once you have made one basic cravat pin, experiment by creating others using your own unique style. Try using different items as centerpieces and adhering them to the pin, in order to increase your technical ability. Be aware of weight when using small pins as bases as they will restrict the adornments you can use. Try experimenting with simple and ornate styles to see which ones you enjoy making the most; take note of the pins that receive the most compliments and build upon those styles.

Tutorial 5: Pocket Watch

To create a pocket watch unique to you, consider whether you want it to be functional or purely decorative. If you're not interested in your watch being operational, you can even create a watch out of other materials, such as photocopying a watch face and laminating it before gluing it to a cardboard base. If you would like your watch to be operational, purchase a functioning pocket watch; often these are available through online auction sites at fairly reasonable prices and can be customized to create a look you like. You can use contrasting colours to decorate your watch – gold, silver and metallics are good colours to use as they give a survivalist feel. You can build a surround to encase your watch if you like, but you will need to make sure your watch is removable to perform maintenance on it. Remember that the battery inside your watch will need to be changed periodically and that you will need to access the mechanism to change the time.

Pocket watches can vary in size and be worn as a necklace or kept in a pocket with an attached chain. If you choose to

Pocket watch.

wear your watch inside a pocket, opt for a larger size as this will sit better inside the space and be visible from outside. Smaller watches lend themselves to being worn as a necklace and can be decorated delicately to complement their size. Depending on the look you would like to portray with your watch, you can opt for a post-apocalyptic grease junkie style with aged metal by using spray paint or acrylics to change the colour, or replicate the more distinguished Victorian time traveller by going for a highly polished finish with plenty of shiny cogs.

For this tutorial you will need:
Pocket watch
Cog
Small key

Tools:
Jewellery adhesive
Round-nosed pliers

Toothpick
Sandpaper or emery board
Cloth or paper towel

Step 1: Take the pocket watch and lay it out onto a flat surface. Arrange the key and cog on a flat area of the watch. Check the placement and try swapping the cog and key around until you're happy. Prepare the surface of the pocket watch. Some pocket watches will have a shiny surface, which will make it difficult to adhere glue to. If your pocket watch's surface is lacking texture, you can provide some by using a coarse-grain sandpaper or emery board. If using an emery board, use the rougher side if it's double-sided. Be careful to only sand small parts of the pocket watch and not all over, as you will only be gluing the cog and key to a small area. Avoid sanding too close to the glass of your watch as you do not want to damage it. If you do have to sand close to it, minimize the risk of damaging the glass by covering it with fabric and holding down with your opposite hand. If you need to use both hands to sand, you can use masking tape to cover the glass. Move the sandpaper back and forth just a few times on a small area and check in between each rub how the texture is developing. Once the metal feels slightly dusty to the touch, it will be texturized enough. Clean away any dust using a dry cloth or paper towel.

Step 2: Use the strong jewellery adhesive to add a small dab of glue to a toothpick. Transfer the glue to the back of the cog or key while holding with the pliers. Press down onto the pocket watch using the dry end of the toothpick. Be sure to press down evenly to avoid slippage. Leave the watch to dry for around twenty minutes so the glue has a chance to superficially bond, before adding the next piece.

Prepare the surface of the pocket watch.

Use the jewellery adhesive to apply the cog to the lid of the watch.

Step 3: Add glue to the back of the key or cog using a toothpick and place on top of the last charm. Press down using the dry end of the toothpick. At this point, should you have any dried glue that has formed on the pocket watch, use the dry end of the toothpick to remove it by dragging it away from under the charms. Leave the watch to dry completely for twenty-four hours until the glue has set.

If you want to decorate the watch more extravagantly, you could add elements to the chain like extra looped chains, bows made from leather, satin or lace, charms, even small glass bottles. If you're not keen on wearing your watch on a chain, you could try making a fob to attach it to. This would look excellent attached to a jacket or even on a top hat.

Glue the key into place.

Most people will know what a jabot is, even if they aren't aware of its correct name. Quite often jabots are confused with cravats. A cravat is a more organic item of neckwear that is dependent for its appearance on the way the wearer ties it. A jabot is an altogether different item, consisting of layers of fabric, normally a medium to heavyweight fabric, that falls in a wave-like style. It is then usually decorated with a cameo, beads or lace.

Jabots can be attached just by pinning the material to your shirt or by attaching the material to a neckband. As most shirts are already equipped with collars, it is sensible to use a piece of elastic to hold your jabot in place. This will make the jabot versatile and wearable with a variety of items, from t-shirts to polo necks. When picking the material for your jabot, try a neutral colour like fawn, cream or black as these will be go with most colours.

As a jabot can be an extravagant piece, it should be designed in an understated fashion to eliminate the chance of it potentially looking too fanciful and spoiling an outfit. To make your jabot look more professional, use the sewing method to attach the fabric. If you're not adept with a needle, however, using fabric glue will keep the items in place for a while. Beware of glue bleeding through fabrics if you decide to do this; lace can be notoriously difficult to glue for this reason. If you decide to use glue, attach a heavier fabric to the band of elastic as a backing and then proceed to glue your lace onto this. This will prevent bleed-through from the glue and add the material weight that is required for the piece to hang correctly.

For this tutorial you will need:
A4-sized sheet of felt in a colour
    similar to the lace colour

2m lace ruffle trim in two different
    colours
1m satin ribbon in a complementary
    colour to the lace trim
Elasticated, thin fabric headband

Tools:
Scissors
Hot glue gun, craft glue or needle and
    thread
Pen
Pattern paper
Dress pins

Step 1: Before beginning to make a jabot, consider the necklines of the outfits you will be wearing it with. If you'll be wearing it with shirts, you'll need to check where the collar begins so that the jabot sits underneath and doesn't push it upwards. Measure the gap between the collar points on the shirt and make a note of it so you can create the right width for the jabot. Using the measurement for the top part of the jabot, draw out a simple wide tie shape onto paper first and cut out the pattern. Hold the pattern up to your shirt and check that the piece will fit well. If the pattern needs adjustments, make a note on the paper and manipulate until it fits the shirt correctly. Use pins to attach the paper pattern to the felt to stop it slipping while drawing around it. At the top part of the pattern, where the neck band will be joined, allow an extra inch to fold over the elastic. This extra inch of material will be used to either sew or glue the band into place. When you're ready, use scissors to cut out the felt pattern.

Step 2: Place the felt onto a flat surface and gather together the two colours of lace trim. The lace will cover the whole of the jabot and will be layered to cover the felt underneath, as well as possible. Unwrap the lace trims and begin to measure them out onto the felt. Start

with the darkest colour first and work from the bottom of the jabot to the top. Measure out the trim along the bottom of the jabot and allow half an inch extra on either side. This will be the allowance to attach to the back of the felt. Be sure to follow the natural curve of the trim. Some trims will fall with a more circular curve, whereas others will be more relaxed. Use the top edge of the trim as a guide to adhere onto the felt. Cut the first piece of trim and use it as a guide. Sequentially cut slightly shorter pieces than the last one until you have enough trim to cover the whole piece of felt, and remember to allow for the important extra allowance to wrap around the back of the felt.

Step 3: Place all the trim out in size order, from large to small. Take the largest piece of trim and lay it across the bottom of the felt. At this point you can decide how you would like to attach your trim, either by using a strong craft glue, hot glue or with a needle and thread. Each has its own benefits and it really does depend on your own personal preference. If you choose to use hot glue, you will save time and can make the jabot very quickly. However, over time, the glue may deteriorate and need resticking in some areas. A strong craft glue will take a long time to dry fully but should withstand the test of time. A needle and thread will be the most time-consuming and fiddly technique but will last indefinitely.

If gluing the trims, add a thin strip of glue to the back of the seam of each piece in turn and press down onto the felt backing, keeping the edges free all the way up the piece, and leaving the top inch free to wrap around the band. Leave to dry completely and then return to glue the back of each edge and tuck neatly around the back of the felt so it is invisible from the front of the jabot and, again, leave to dry completely. If using a

Jabot.

needle and thread, use a running stitch to attach the trims using the top edge. Secure each piece of trim in turn by stitching all the way around so the ends are tucked neatly behind the jabot and tie off the thread to finish.

Step 4: Next, take the satin ribbon. Ideally, choose a wide piece of ribbon as this will be used to create the bow for the jabot, allowing it to look large and full. Lay the ribbon out along a flat surface and locate the centre point by taking one end and pulling it over till it touches the other end. The centre point will be located in the middle of the loop on the opposite end. Insert a dress pin through the centre point of the ribbon to mark its place. Pick the ribbon up and place it on the jabot with the centre point touching the top layer of lace trim. Make sure the ribbon is below the bare top inch of felt. Glue the ribbon into place and leave to dry for a short while or stitch into place using just a few stitches at the centre point. The ribbon needs to have enough

movement to enable it to be tied, so the less material attached to the jabot, the better. The ribbon must be securely attached to make sure it has enough structural stability to stay in place.

Step 5: Next, take the elasticated headband and locate the metal securing clip. Place the metal clip towards the back so it will be hidden by the collar of the shirt. Take the jabot and fold the top inch of felt over the band. Check that the felt wraps around the band completely and touches the felt on the underside of the jabot. Keep the elasticated band flat and make sure it's not twisted as that will cause the jabot to sit higher on one side and also push the collar outwards. When everything is in place, stitch or glue the felt over the band so it is secure. Leave the glue to dry fully before continuing to the next step.

Step 6: Tie the ribbon into a large bow and position the loose ends so that they hang downwards on either side of the

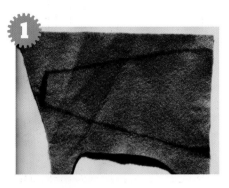

Create the felt template and cut out.

Cut the trims till you have enough to cover the felt.

Attach the pieces of trim to the felt from the bottom to the top and make sure you tuck the ends behind the felt.

Glue the satin ribbon to the top of the jabot.

Attach the felt to the neck band.

Tie the bow and shape the ends.

jabot. You may need to try tying the bow a few different times until you're happy with the look of it. When the bow is in place, snip an upside down 'V' shape into either end of the length of ribbon. Seal the ends with a lighter to prevent them from fraying. Be careful to keep the flame well away from the jabot and lift the ends of the ribbons up and away from the lace. Pass the lighter over the ends of the ribbon quickly, no more than half a second on each side. This should be enough to seal the ends thoroughly. Should at any point the ribbon catch fire, blow the flame out and wait for a few seconds before touching the end of the ribbon as it will be very hot. When working with flames, be sensible and make sure you have water to hand, just in case things get out of hand. As long as you follow the instructions carefully and keep flammable items away from the lighter, there is little to no risk.

Once you have finished the piece, place it around your collar and fluff the lace ruffles up until they look full. If you're not too keen on the bow at the top of the jabot, you can wear it in more of a tucked tie style. Play around with different positionings of the bow until you're happy with the placement. Try wearing the jabot with other types of clothing such as a waistcoat and t-shirt. If you would like to cover the elastic neckband, use a scarf or a piece of ribbon to place over the top. This will disguise the band and make it look like a cravat.

When you're not wearing your jabot, store it somewhere where it won't suffer from being flattened. To wash your jabot, use a damp sponge containing a small amount of laundry detergent with a very small amount of water. Felt will suffer if it gets wet and, depending on the base material it is made from, it can shrink. Always fully air-dry the jabot after washing and before storing.

Chapter 9
Putting an Outfit Together on the Cheap

There are mysteries which men can only guess at, which age by age they may solve only in part.
– BRAM STOKER

Steampunk can be an expensive genre to be part of when it comes to purchasing clothing. There are many ways you can put together an outfit with next to no money, upcycling being one of them. The art of upcycling is to take items that may otherwise be discarded and to repurpose them into something better than the original. Upcycling will undoubtedly save you money, but it takes time to create a new item from another piece.

When looking to upcycle an item, it is best to first sketch out the final design before you start working to it. This is particularly important when upcycling garments as you must avoid making a mistake that can't be rectified, such as removing a piece of fabric which is essential to the cut or fall of the piece. Use existing items in your wardrobe for ideas so you create a more cohesive collection of items that will gel well together. When putting an outfit together, start with just the basic items such as a skirt and shirt or trousers. You can then begin to build upon these with accessories and outer garments that will complement your new pieces.

Steampunk Fabrics

Steampunk has a few regularly used fabrics that should become part of your staple style. Brocade, silk, chiffon and velvet are a few easily recognizable and common materials that will make up most of your outfits already. But Steampunk style should not be limited to these fabrics alone and there are many other cheaper alternatives that can be used just as effectively and with just as much of an opulent air to them.

Heavy fabrics such as those often used for upholstery are an excellent choice for larger, more striking items such as outer garments, skirts or trousers, as they will stand up to the wear and tear of everyday life and will wear well over time. Opt for tweeds, leather and coloured denims (avoid the usual blue hues) as these will sit nicely due to their weight, and they work well as part of an outfit containing lighter fabrics such as chiffons and silks.

Use fabrics to your advantage by teaming contrasting textures, colours and patterns. Pairing patterns together will require some experimentation on your part in order to get the correct combination, but once you have made a few mistakes you will then know what

patterns you like together and what works best for you. Stripes and florals marry well, as do filigree and lace, but it's also worth trying combinations that may not necessarily seem compatible, as the results can create something unexpectedly perfect and unique.

Accessories Maketh the Ensemble

Accessories are an obvious choice when trying to add new life to your wardrobe. They are versatile, can be easy to make, and can turn an ordinary outfit into something extraordinary. Picking accessories should be based on a few factors and these factors will change from outfit to outfit but will usually remain fairly similar. Make your choices based on what you would like to wear, not what you think you should wear. Ultimately, your choices should be based upon your own style and this will shine through in the accessories you pick. Make your colour selections wisely and clash and contrast with accessories if you wish as this will make them stand out. If you decide to clash colours, pick hues that are decidedly different from each other rather than closely related

LEFT: Steampunk outfit.

Steampunk hair style. (Charis Talbot Photography)

shades, as these will create confusion in your pigment choices.

Layer jewellery such as necklaces, bracelets, rings and cuffs only when your outfit is simple, using plain unpatterned clothing. Layering too much jewellery can seem brash and gauche, particularly on top of a highly detailed pattern. Hair pieces, fascinators and millinery will be enough of a statement on their own; keep other accessories minimal when wearing headgear. Other accessories such as shoes and belts should be in neutral colours unless you wish to make them a statement piece as part of your outfit.

Hair Tips

When it comes to styling your hair, you can spend five minutes creating a beautifully simple updo or a few hours working through a style using tongs, pins and products. It really is down to personal preference and working with your own skills. If you want to stick with what is easily achievable but also well executed, use simple styles that aren't too far out of your comfort zone.

Clothing often does the talking in Steampunk, so hairstyles are usually kept fairly plain. It pays to do some research into hairstyles from the Victorian and Edwardian periods as these styles are often replicated. Hair is usually left long and tousled in loose waves or basic curls. If your hair is able to hold a curl, use curling tongs to create this look and shake tight curls out into loose waves, or sleep in tight curlers overnight so they drop out into softer locks.

Plaits and braids can be used to keep hair away from the face, but keep them loose and slightly messy to emulate the hardworking Victorian woman or time-travelling dame. Backcombed tresses which have been styled into a low bun or split into two and piled messily upon the

head are also popular and make for a perfect texturized base for hats and fascinators to nestle into. If you're not able to curl your hair then bunches are also a preferred style and will look positively post-apocalyptic with a touch of backcombing on the lower sections.

Most Steampunk hairstyles require hair that's quite long; shorter hair is not usually considered in most style guides. There are, however, a few options for those with shorter hair who want to create a Steampunk look. Really short hair can be cut into an elfin-style crop, given lots of choppy texture and accessorized with some futuristic goggles or a fascinator. This will give a more modern look as opposed to the traditional historical styles.

To create the longer styles with shorter hair, you can use extensions, half-wigs or hairpieces. These can be bought online fairly inexpensively and in a variety of colours to match your own. Should you wish to have the option to change the texture of the hairpiece, wig or extensions, it is best to purchase human hair. Human hair will last for a long time and is completely versatile. It can be straightened, washed, curled, dyed and treated almost as you would treat your own hair, with the added flexibility of being able to be styled away from the head. Some synthetic extensions can also be treated this way but not with quite so many options. The styling process can be tough on synthetic extensions and most aren't compatible with heat. Check labels thoroughly before purchasing to make sure that the extensions are suitable for your style plans.

A lot of synthetic hair extensions have an unnatural shine to them, which makes them stand out too obviously from your own natural hair. To remove the shine quickly, spray some dry shampoo onto the lengths of the extensions and brush through. This will temporarily add

texture and remove some of the shine. To remove the shine from the extensions permanently, add one capful of fabric softener to a bucket and add another capful of water. Leave the extensions to soak in the water for three to five days. If the extensions have clips attached, be sure to leave them outside the bucket so they don't rust, or place them securely inside a rubber glove and secure the opening with a rubber band to prevent water entering. Keep checking the extensions over the following days until they start to look less shiny.

When the desired look is achieved, take the hair extensions out of the container and wash through in the shower until the fabric softener has been fully removed. Leave to dry naturally and then gently style the extensions into the style you require, being careful to follow the styling guidelines supplied with them. Soaking the extensions shouldn't remove the styling if they're made from synthetic hair, but they may need shaking out afterwards to return them to their original shape. The same technique shouldn't be used with human hair extensions as it could ruin them. Human hair extensions can be dulled by using dry shampoo.

Other shorter or mid-length styles can be easily styled to look longer by very loosely tucking hair around an elasticated hair band in a twisted roll fashion known as a Gibson and pinned at the back using jewelled barrettes. Spray the style lightly with hairspray to finish. This style is well suited to a Decopunk outfit and adds real elegance to an outfit. It is also quite often used for bridal hair and emulates styles that were popular in the 1920s. More inspiration for shorter styles can be found online and it's worth checking cosplay websites, as these will have inspirational images and also a list of suppliers selling suitable hair accessories, wigs and extensions.

Hair can be coloured any shade you are partial to: natural shades such as dark brown and honey blonde are favoured, along with brighter unnatural shades like platinum blonde and scarlet; even tangerine can be a striking choice. Personal preference and research should be considered when deciding to make a drastic colour change, along with planning around your wardrobe to avoid any major colour clashes. Choose hair dyes that are vibrant and will care for your hair. Vegetable-based dyes are kind to hair and semi-permanent, which allows for more frequent colour changes if needed. For more permanent colouring consult with your hairdresser to deliver the result you require, unless you're confident and experienced with colouring your own hair at home.

You can use fascinators, hairbands, clips, barrettes and hats, amongst other items of headgear, to emphasize hairstyles. If you're wearing headgear, be sure to keep your hairstyle understated unless you wish to go for a more futuristic mad professor style, in which case big curls or sculpted updos will look exceptional. When wearing headgear, consider that some items may be heavy so will require further support to avoid tugging on your hair. This can be done by adding clip-in hair extensions so that the weight of the headpiece is taken by the extensions and not your own hair. You can create extra padding for hair and create rolls by using bun rings cut in half to provide strips to wrap your own hair around. These create volume but are also an excellent anchoring device for larger fascinators when pinned with hair grips or bobby pins.

When choosing styling products for hair, it is worth thinking of the overall style you wish to emulate. For post-apocalyptic, retro-futurism hair, you need to create texture and less polished styles than those of the Victorian-inspired Steampunk style. Try using dry shampoo or beach sprays, which can be bought from most chemists but are also easily made at home: use a spray bottle filled three-quarters full with warm water, three teaspoons of sea salt, two tablespoons of coconut oil, one teaspoon of conditioner and a teaspoon of gel, and shake together. Spray this through towel-dried hair and leave to dry naturally to give natural yet beautifully textured hair that is easy to style.

For more polished Victorian-inspired styles, try to use as little product as possible. Styles should look clean and mainly rely on pins to hold hair in place. Use a small amount of product such as mousse throughout damp hair and blow dry to give hair a styleable touch of texture. This will make sure hair remains in place without looking too over-styled or weighed down with product. To finish styles, use a small amount of shine spray or hairspray to hold in place.

Men's hair should be kept neat and tidy; refer to men's styles from the Victorian or Edwardian period or ask your barber to replicate a 'high and tight' hairstyle, which is a closely shaved side with a longer top, usually worn with a side parting. Ask him to cut the sides of your hair so they're tapered. This will ensure that any hair showing under hats is neat and tapers towards the neck. If you prefer to wear your hair longer, make sure it is kept conditioned and looks smooth and tidy. If holding long hair in a ponytail, make sure you don't team it with a hat that will squash it down. Instead, try goggles or a hat tipped to the front. You can plait a ponytail from the nape of the neck downwards and this will leave the back of the hair flat for wearing a hat.

Depending on the look you're trying to achieve – whether it's Victorian traditional, Dieselpunk or Decopunk – try to theme your hair to go with your outfit. If you're trying to emulate a mad professor, it would be fun to leave a few strands of hair out of place to give the illusion you've been hard at work in the lab. If you are trying to channel a post-apocalyptic style, try spraying some dry shampoo into your hair to create a dusty look. Whatever sub-genre of Steampunk you're trying to create, there will be a way of theming your hairstyle to match.

Don't be afraid to try styles out before committing to them. A wilder hairstyle can be worn if you are feeling daring, but keep any headgear to a minimum as you don't want your head to look overcrowded. Natural hair colours are preferable as they replicate the styles from historical references. However, if hair is coloured in bright hues, this can also be a good contrast to many outfits and make them more distinguishable. A classic Victorian style, dyed in a bright colour, gives the wearer a futuristic look and this makes an excellent style to team with a post-apocalyptic look.

Should you wish to have the fun of a bright colour but cannot commit to it for full-time wear, purchase temporary colour sprays or gels. Colour sprays have really improved in quality over the last few years, changing from their costume counterparts, which tended to coat the hair with a hard chalky paste, to now being touchable and soft. There are now many good products on the market available in a multitude of colours and they're relatively inexpensive to buy. The beauty of temporary products means that they will last for the amount of time that you need them but, as soon as you have to be ready for the office, you can wash them out and return your hair to its natural shade.

To style hair, you can use products such as pomades for short dos and a shine spray for longer hair. Hairspray is also a good all-round product that can be used to seal styles in place and stop them from moving. With hair products, less is most definitely more; always use less than you think you need and then add if you need more. You want to avoid hair that is full of product as it will look weighed down and over-styled.

Men should try to theme any facial hair towards the look they're trying to achieve. For a classic Steampunk look, beards and moustaches should be trimmed, even and neat. For a more post-apocalyptic style, try adding colour to your beard or adding some dry shampoo to make it look as if you've been through a war.

Regardless of the look you're trying to achieve, you should always take care of your facial hair for your own comfort. Beard oils and moustache waxes are all fairly readily available from high street chemists, as facial hair has had a huge resurgence in popularity in recent years. Beard oils and waxes will allow you to condition your facial hair so it is soft and pliable, making it more comfortable against your skin. Wax will allow you to style your beard so it is held in shape, and moustaches can be shaped into a style of your choice.

If you wish to make a feature of your facial hair, it is worth investing in a specially made beard comb and moustache trimming kit. Some kits are beautifully presented in a vintage style, which will go nicely with any outfits you choose to wear; the decorated tins look rather attractive poking out of a waistcoat pocket. Most classic Steampunk looks feature the curled moustache. This requires growing some length to your moustache and, using a styling comb, brushing the moustache to either side with a parting in the centre of your lip. Then gently twirl the ends around with your fingers to create the loops at either end. Always carry a small pot of wax with you, as throughout the day your beard may become untidy or your moustache may uncurl, and you can use the wax to top up your look and make sure you always look distinguished

and not dishevelled.

Shoes and Customizing

There are plenty of pre-made Steampunk shoes available on the internet and sometimes on sale in the high street. Some of these shoes are very well made and the quality will be reflected in their price; some are not so well made and this, sadly, is not always reflected in their price. It is best to research brands that others recommend and have used themselves. You can procure this information easily through Steampunk online forums and by searching for reputable brands. Of course, if you wish to purchase ready-made shoes, this is a fast time-saving option but can be costly. Customizing a pair of shoes you already own is an excellent way to ensure you have something exclusive in your collection.

There are a multitude of ways to customize shoes, many requiring a considerable amount of time and patience. Firstly, you should choose the type of shoes you would like to work on. If you're using fabric shoes such as canvas, these are best suited to customizing with paint or by sewing fabrics onto the outers. If you decide to use leather or plastic shoes, you will need to use strong glue to hold any accoutrements firmly on the foundation of the shoe.

When decorating your footwear, bear in mind how you will be wearing it. If your shoes are for everyday wear, paints are advisable with a coat of spray varnish or similar to coat the shoes and stop them chipping. If painting onto fabric, make sure your shoes are backed with a protective lining such as baking paper or cellophane until dry to prevent paint leaking onto the fabric underneath. You can paint your shoes with anything you like – cogs, filigree, stripes. Be creative and use your own

sense of style to come up with ideas.

Fabric paints come in many guises and are quite a versatile medium. There are fabric paints that puff up on fabrics to create a raised effect, which are ideal if you're going for a 3D or layered look. Fabric pens provide fantastic precision and are easily workable around spaces like laces and heels. Standard fabric paints will require some skill to use. Use templates and stencils if you're not particularly steady with a paintbrush, as this will create crisp and neat lines.

A way to customize shoes without painting or having to add anything to them is by using spats or gaiters. Spats are a type of shoe cover that look like the top of a boot. They can vary in length but always cover the foot from just below the ankle and to the top of the foot. They were originally invented to protect the ankles and shoes from the filthy streets, when horses were used as the only form of transport. Spatterdashes, as they were known, were worn by those in higher society and were seen as an important part of daily dress for most men in the late nineteenth century; they remained a popular part of fashion until the 1930s.

Spats then began to disappear from the feet of the upper classes, though no one knows why. It is thought that with the invention of the modern motor vehicle and the development of roads, they were no longer required to protect footwear from the splashes of puddles and mud. Spats in their first incarnation were usually made of thick fabrics that were easy to clean. Nowadays they can be made from many materials but are usually created in leather as this is hardwearing and suitable for all weathers. They are also available in various fabrics and also, more unusually, in latex.

Spats can be fastened by buttoning them down the side, or attached with straps under the arch of the foot and around the ankle. They can also be made using elasticated materials that require the wearer to pull them onto the foot. You can either make your own spats by purchasing a pattern and fabric and sewing them together yourself, or you can buy them ready-made. Consider where you will be wearing them when choosing your material. If you require your spats to be weatherproof, choose a fabric that will withstand the wet. If your spats are purely for aesthetic wear, choose a fabric that you find pleasing and make them from this.

Spats can be difficult to find ready-made but online craft shops such as Etsy will feature designers that make them. This way you can purchase direct from a designer and they may be able to process a customized pair especially for you.

Corsets, Harnesses and Bustles

Corsets

If you're looking to create an exceptional 'historical' Steampunk costume, corsets, harnesses and bustles are an ideal choice as they will give your outfit the required air of authenticity. Corsets have seen a revival in recent years as they are now being used for their waist-reducing capabilities. Currently, the most popular modern corsets resemble traditional medical corsets, which are used by those needing protection after surgery or by sufferers of long-term spinal injuries. This is because medical corsets are made for long-term wear and are more comfortable than their traditional counterparts.

Corsets can vary enormously in quality and price. Specialist handmade corsets are the most exquisite items of costumery, but the hours spent making them is reflected in their cost. At the opposite end of the scale, there are very cheap corsets which should be avoided at all costs. Cheaper corsets will bend and can cause painful bruising or rub

on the skin. This is due to the type of boning used. Boning is the structured element of a corset – the struts that give your corset shape and keep it rigid. Cheap boning is usually made from plastic and will inevitably bend, leaving you with an unwearable corset which will fold when worn. A mid-range corset from a specialist corset manufacturer will be a good investment and can be worn repeatedly.

If you purchase a corset in a neutral colour, it can be worn over or under clothing and with a range of outfits. Avoid buying a corset without first trying it on as your corset should fit your shape perfectly. There are a few different designs of corset and these should all be considered for their various merits and flaws before you make your purchase. Longline corsets can be desirable if you wish to elongate your torso and improve your pelvic shape. Longline corsets are a more traditional Edwardian style, whereas standard length corsets are indicative of the Victorian period. Standard length corsets allow the wearer more freedom of movement and are not as restrictive as longline corsets. They are also a sensible choice if you wish to wear your corset as outerwear as they can be layered over skirts and worn with a bustle. Longline corsets can be worn with bustles but only if the bustle is worn over the corset, as they obscure the waist band where the bustle usually sits.

Corsets should be worn with care and never for more than a few hours at a time. If corsets are worn incorrectly for longer periods of time, they can cause bruising to the skin or, in the worst cases, damage to the internal organs. When deciding to wear a corset for the first time, do plenty of research on how to do this properly without causing harm to yourself. Wearing a corset for a few hours should cause you no harm but it's advisable, to start with, to build your resistance by wearing your corset in

twenty-minute increments; this will prepare your body slowly and safely for longer sessions.

To begin, wear your corset loosely laced. You should feel a slight pressure around your body but you shouldn't experience any pain. If your corset becomes painful to wear, loosen the lacing and reduce the amount of time you wear it. Once you have trained your waist, it is possible to get a reasonable reduction around your middle. This will give you the desired hourglass silhouette that is deemed appealing in Steampunk circles. Your corset will also be more comfortable to wear if you take your time with waist training.

Harnesses

A Steampunk harness is a simple way to add a mechanical feel to an outfit. Harnesses evoke an era of mechanical engineering, conjuring imagery of leather aprons and garments used to keep clothing away from work benches. They have seen a huge increase in popularity over the last year and have been used on catwalks around the world and worn by many famous pop stars. The harness has become a surefire way to add a more alternative look to something more feminine. Many dresses have recently featured caging harnesses attached to dresses as part of the design. These are usually juxtaposed with floral motifs to create a soft look with a hard edge. The humble harness should be a simplistic item and used to accentuate an outfit. Wearing a harness over a plain black t-shirt paired with goggles, jeans and boots creates a dressed-down version of Steampunk that is quick and easy to replicate for an everyday look.

Harnesses can be made in a variety of styles, from simple strap designs using just a small amount of material or other items to create the basic shape, to more intricate ones such as a waistcoat style

A decorative corset. (Charis Talbot Photography)

that uses more material. Some harnesses can be made by using found accessories and joining them together. For example, attaching three belts together with the use of some leather tools and eyelets can create a rather rustic-looking harness in next to no time. However, if you wish to create something more fanciful, you can cut and create a pattern and stitch this together using a heavy-duty sewing machine that can handle leather, or you could hand-sew one. As harnesses are usually small, hand-sewing should be sufficient as it won't take an extraordinary amount of time to complete. You may wish to line a harness if you plan to wear it over clothing or on bare skin, as it will protect you from any potential chafing.

Patterns for harnesses can be found online and some websites will offer basic patterns for free, which can keep costs down. A heavy fabric will suit a harness best as it will replicate the protective nature of the garment. Using rivets will give your harness more of a mechanical feel and patterns can be made using a leather punch and an eyelet tool. Shapes can be cut from leather and glued to a harness if you wish to create a more theatrical look. Shapes such as cogs, insects and feathers all make good Steampunk appliqués, but use your own sense of style to make something unique to you.

Should you wish to purchase a pre-made harness, there are a few designers around who specialize in leather work and their pieces are exquisitely made. Other designers use fabric for their harnesses and these can be a softer everyday alternative to leather.

When not wearing your harness, it is important to care for it properly. Store leather away from moisture and in a sealed airtight container. Purchase a few silica gel packs and place these inside the container as they will absorb any moisture that may penetrate the leather

and cause it to deteriorate or become mouldy. Remember that leather is a natural product and can deteriorate quickly if not looked after properly. Be sure to polish as well as condition the leather before you wear it as this will ensure the harness becomes supple and weather resistant. A good leather conditioner can be purchased for a reasonable price and used every few months.

If your harness becomes dirty, wash very gently with saddle soap and only apply to the outer layer of the material to avoid it becoming waterlogged. Leave the leather to dry at room temperature overnight and then condition. When leather has been washed, it may require a bit more conditioner to get it back to its original flexibility. Apply the conditioner and leave for a few hours or overnight to sink into the skin and wipe the excess away the next day using a paper towel. This should leave your leather in excellent condition and will make it incredibly durable. Once the leather has been conditioned, you can then add a small amount of polish. Polish should be used sparingly to add the slightest shine to the piece; too much polish can darken leather and make it look unhealthy. Repeat these steps to care for your harness when the leather is looking a little dull and it should last a lifetime.

Bustles

A bustle is a garment that is designed to accentuate the posterior of a dress by pushing it out to make a more defined shape, leaving the front of the dress straight. It was originally designed to be worn underneath a large, long-length skirt, but bustles can also be worn over the top of clothing.

The bustle we are familiar with today came about after clothing became sleeker and hooped skirts were falling

out of fashion. An attachable bustle that was tied at the waist, usually with a decorative bow, was created to give more comfort to the wearer. It was designed to create the required large look of a hooped skirt but without the weight. This made it easier for the wearer to sit down: she simply lifted the bustle up and dropped it over the back of a chair. As the attachable bustle became more popular, dresses were designed to have a flap of material that covered a cage-type bustle. This slowly eliminated the fashion for hooped skirts and, heading into the Edwardian era, skirts became much more sleek and streamlined.

Nowadays bustles worn outside clothing are usually made from materials such as netting or tulle, which is bunched together to give a ruched and bulbous appearance. Bustles should be highly decorative and include elements such as bows or a train, a piece of material that hangs at the mid-length of the original skirt or longer. Luxurious materials should be used for the decorative parts of the bustle to create the air of opulence it requires.

Bustles can also be made in the form of a three-quarters full skirt, by using a bustle pattern that contains a curtain-type front. Patterns for historical garments can be purchased from specialist retailers and are worth buying as they contain some very handy shapes. Historical patterns often adapt original shapes and make them usable for today. For example, most modern historical patterns will have been created with the maker in mind, using modern equipment such as a sewing machine.

Use a heavyweight fabric such as velvet, satin or tweed as a base material for your bustle. This will ensure the bustle hangs correctly and looks high-end.

If you don't want to make a bustle yourself, you can purchase one from a few shops that specialize in more gothic-style clothing or bridal wear. It is advisable to buy it in a setting where you can get a feel for it. This will allow you to check if it is good quality and will sit correctly. Some bustles are made with cheaper materials, particularly when it comes to burlesque bustles. These bustles are made for show and not for wearing for long periods of time. Stay away from bustles that contain tulle to carry out the bulk of the padding; these will flatten quickly and can become uneven when wearing, leaving you with an uneven silhouette. A good quality bustle will contain caging made from plastic or steel boning and may also contain tulle, but that shouldn't be the main padding fabric. The caging makes a solid, light and flexible shape that will maintain its silhouette. This will provide you with a good outline to your outfit that won't require constant adjustment.

When purchasing or making a bustle, you should consider what clothing you will be wearing it with as it will need to be in a matching colour or similar colour palette. Bustles should be a neutral colour such as beige, cream, gold, black or brown, so they can be teamed with many different skirts or dresses. Creating an attachable cage which can be placed under a matching flap of material will make it easier to interchange the bustle for different outfits and will make it cheaper than buying a new bustle each time. You can wear a bustle with a variety of outfits, not just dresses. If you really want to make an impact, wearing a bustle over trousers or jeans and paired with boots creates a truly unique look that adds an air of modernity to a historical fashion item.

Conclusion

We should strive to welcome change and challenges, because they are what help us grow. Without them we grow weak like the Eloi in comfort and security. We need to constantly be challenging ourselves in order to strengthen our character and increase our intelligence.
— H.G. WELLS, *THE TIME MACHINE*

Making jewellery successfully takes many hours of practice. By going over your techniques and taking time to perfect what you have learned, you will become a proficient jewellery maker. Try to be methodical when learning and don't get overwhelmed by trying to juggle too many new techniques. Perfect one technique at a time and if you're struggling to pick up a new skill, step away for a small break and try again. The learning process should be fun and exciting; if at any point you find yourself becoming frustrated or distracted, try and dissect what it is that's not working. Once you have had some time to think about the problem, usually a solution will form and you will be back on your way.

As you develop your skills, try where possible to input your own personality into the resulting product. When following the material lists, choose items such as fabrics that are personal to you or which could be made for others. Once you have practised the techniques in this book, you will find that some techniques work for you personally and some will be more difficult to master. The more you forge your own way within jewellery-making styles, the quicker you will find your own niche and develop your own techniques.

Try experimenting when creating items and make sure you document what went well and what didn't. This will help you further down the line when you want to make items using your own designs. Try something new every time you make a design; experiment and build upon your knowledge to create unique items that will be special to you. The more you try things out and succeed, the more likely you will expand and build on your techniques.

A lot of the magic of jewellery-making is in the sketching and design stage. From this point, you can think about how to facilitate a set of personal techniques which won't be easily replicated. This will be a first step to designing small, unique, cohesive collections.

Struggling and failing can be frustrating when making jewellery, but it is an important part of the learning process. Without failure, there is limited opportunity to learn from the mistakes that are made. Mistakes can be made in everything from technique to material choices. Trial and error will be your biggest asset when learning the craft, especially when it comes to materials. Some materials will seem like the perfect choice at the time, but when it comes to using them for their intended purpose

they may not work. Although this can be disappointing and costly at the time, it is important not to be disheartened but to note down what didn't work so that you create your own reference library to work from. Try noting mistakes down as you work so you don't forget them later. Also, take time to note down what works well and the projects you enjoy making the most. These will form a good basis for things to make in the future.

Try to gain feedback from others about the projects you have made to highlight what people do and don't like about them. Constructive criticism is helpful at an early stage as it will help you see your designs from another perspective and point of view. Try asking people who are creative-minded about your designs but also those who are self-confessed non-creatives. You will find that you receive entirely different critiques but both will be valid and helpful. Try not to take criticism personally. This can be easier said than done when you have put so much of your own personality into a design, but remember that criticism is only one person's opinion and you don't have to necessarily agree with that viewpoint — but take elements of the critique and use them to gain outsider knowledge.

LEFT: Develop your own style.

Steampunk Style

By taking your time and working through the projects in the book, you will be growing and gaining skills along the way. Making Steampunk jewellery is more about the choices you make in the design process than becoming fantastic at technical skill, even though you will need a small amount to get by. Learning to work on projects systematically and keeping many ideas in mind for projects in the future will really help you build your Steampunk style. By collaborating with others, discussing ideas, and using plenty of research and inspiration, you can create many varied and exciting projects which will be unique to you and your style. Build upon what you find intriguing and exciting within Steampunk and beyond. You will be able to exceed the boundaries of what you originally thought would be possible within your designs if you keep trying to create astounding items.

Following the projects set out in the book will enable you to complete some exciting jewellery challenges, which will help to build your skill set and knowledge. Should you find you reach a stage where you have progressed to wanting to sell your work to the public, make sure you price items fairly to reflect the cost of materials, time and effort put into the piece. All too often items are underpriced and this can devalue your work. There is plenty of information and debate about how to correctly price items for individual sale and for wholesale on online craft forums. These make interesting and informative reading and will give you an insight into how to begin valuing your work.

The most important piece of advice for a new maker to embrace is to be proud of your work. Often designers and creatives actively take steps to point out flaws in their work, undervaluing its worth and ultimately belittling their own efforts. Be positive about your creations, but also realistic. If something isn't looking or sitting correctly, make minor adjustments to improve designs. Try stepping back from your creations to look at them with fresh eyes. You're bound to see some minor imperfections or mistakes, but ignore them and remember that 'handmade' and 'unique' is much more intriguing and beguiling than 'mass produced'.

Much like Steampunk, innovation and exploration should be at the heart of all your creations. Should you find yourself struggling at any point and floundering, remember why you began making pieces and be inspired to continue. Creating items that have sentimental and emotional connections will make them timeless and personal to you and others. This is a sure-fire way to make your work interesting and a talking point. Jewellery-making should evoke some passion and spirit and not just be a style choice. Of course, making items that are purely aesthetic is wonderful and can be truly liberating, but this is not possible without at least some base-level emotional connection to the material, item or style that you have chosen.

Steampunk is an emotionally evocative style and provides a basis for developing stories in your items. Whole collections could be formed around a particular story of your own imagining or perhaps a real-life adventure. Taking time to immerse yourself fully into the Steampunk world when creating pieces will result in authenticity and deliver a true, well considered, thought-out design.

Through creating the projects within this book, I hope that you can develop, grow and bloom into a fully fledged jewellery-maker. Regardless of the style your skills eventually lead you to, keep practising, make notes, smile through failure and value your creations as perfect, despite imperfection.

Further Information

You may be brand new to the Steampunk genre or perhaps you've been championing Steampunk for a long while. Wherever you are in your Steampunk journey, you can always learn more to help with the authenticity of your style or perhaps to just increase your knowledge or even just for fun. There are many great fun activities that happen along side the Steampunk genre, for example, there are a few Steampunk conventions and weekenders which are worth researching to see if any are within your reach.

There is also Steampunk music and bands who may be playing shows near you and there may be Steampunk interest groups who meet up near you. If you're not able to get out and about or simply do not have the time, then the internet is a great way to meet people through mutual interest groups and forums.

YouTube has a wealth of Steampunk videos for your viewing pleasure from everything from make-up looks, ray gun tutorials and documentaries on the Steampunk movement.

Steampunk is a heavily literary-influenced genre so it's worth looking into some of the leaders in this field. Some authors are more historical influencers of the genre and others more modern day authentics.

I've listed a few suggestions of authors, bands, etc. that I enjoy and that I have found useful in defining my Steampunk knowledge. Some of these things may not be for you and that's ok. Steampunk isn't a 'one size fits all' genre and I encourage you to do your own research to find out what you may like yourself but also to further your education if you already enjoy the Steampunk genre. You may wish to have a casual overview and just use Steampunk to influence your style in small increments or you may go all out and design your whole home with a Steampunk interior. However you decide to use Steampunk in your everyday life, hopefully the websites listed on the following pages will take you to something new and exciting.

Pinterest

Pinterest is an innovative website where users can create visual boards using any available visual content from the whole of the glorious world wide web. Use Pinterest to create boards for everything to do with interior design, tutorial ideas, clothing or go wild and let you imagination do the choosing.
http://www.pinterest.com

Steampunk and Science Fiction/Fantasy Authors of Note

Historical

H.G. Wells, Jules Verne , Mary Shelley

Modern

K.W. Jetter, William Gibson and Bruce Sterling, Tim Powers, Cherie Priest, Jim Butcher, Gail Carriger, Lee Tisler, Karina Cooper

Films with Steampunk Inspiration

Suckerpunch, Time After Time, The League Of Extraordinary Gentlemen, Adele Blanc Sec, Wild Wild West, Solomon Kane, 9, Snowpiercer

Steampunk Characters, Influencers, Illustrators and Designers

Brian Kesinger, Thomas Willeford, Jake Von Slatt, Kate 'Kato' Lambert

Steampunk Musicians and Bands

Abney Park, Professor Elemental, Steam Powered Giraffe, Doctor Steel, The Men That Will Not Be Blamed For Nothing, Frenchy The Punk

Graphic Novels and Comic Writers

Kia Asamiya, Doug TenNapel, Alan Moore & Kevin O'Neill , Bryan Talbot, Lea Hernandez

Steampunk Online Forums

Steampunk Empire
http://www.thesteampunkempire.com/

Brass Goggles, Steampunk News

Steampunk Events

Steampunk World's Fair
Asylum Steampunk Festival
Wild West Steampunk Convention

List of Suppliers

Jewellery Suppliers

Leander Ornaments
Unique pendants ornaments and supplies.https://www.etsy.com/uk/shop/LeanderOrnaments

Dime Store Emporium
Jewellery supplies and adornments.
https://www.etsy.com/uk/shop/dimestoreemporium

Umbrella Laboratory
Steampunk goggles, jewellery supplies and accoutrements.
https://www.etsy.com/uk/shop/UmbrellaLaboratory

Crafty Bird Decoden
Decoden and other craft supplies.
https://www.etsy.com/uk/shop/CraftybirdDecoden

Cameo Jewelry Supply
Cameos, lockets, frames and other jewellery supplies.
https://www.etsy.com/uk/shop/cameojewelrysupply

Steampunk Clothing and Accessory Suppliers

Steampunk Couture
Neo-Victorian, sci-fi and shabby chic fashion.
http://www.Steampunkcouture.com

Mardigan Enterprises
Adornments and gadgetry.
https://www.etsy.com/shop/MardiganEnterprises

Damsel in this Dress
Steampunk clothing and accessories for women.
http://www.damseldress.com

Fan plus Friend
Gothic, neo-Victorian Steampunk clothing for women.
http://www.fanplusfriend.com

Steampunk Threads
Steampunk clothing, footwear and accessories for men and women.
http://www.fanplusfriend.com

Gentlemans Emporium
Historical reproduction clothing for men and women.
http://www.gentlemansemporium.com

Devine Delinquents
Steampunk, gothic and alternative handmade jewellery and accessories.
https://www.etsy.com/uk/shop/DevineDelinquents

Punkrave Clothing
An unusual mix of beautifully well crafted unique clothing items. One of the leaders in Steampunk and Gothic couture style clothing. Particularly good for men's clothing.

Chic Star
Excellent selection of women's Steampunk coats and jackets amongst other garments. Plus size also catered for at reasonable prices.

Aderlass
German online store specializing in more Gothic-themed clothing, but also offers a few Steampunk staples for both men and women.

Alternative Footwear
A one-stop shop for all your footwear needs. Stocks styles for all genders with a wide range of sizes and styles.

Banned Apparel
Occasional Steampunk gems pop up within this female clothing brand. This is a wholesale website but stockists are listed so you'll be able to find somewhere which will stock near you or an online store that is able to ship to you.

Devil Inspired
Lolita and retro-inspired women's clothing with some Steampunk gems also listed.

Necessary Evil Clothing

Tailors to prestigious Gothic bands such as Lacuna Coil. Stockists of both men and women's clothing. Reasonably priced for stocking up on basics.

T.U.K. Shoes

A great place to pick up reasonably priced, well-made shoes. Styles here vary, but very good for basic trainers for wearing with more dressed down outfits or platform mary-janes to team with skirts.

Steampunk Decor

West Ninth Vintage

Lighting and home decor.
https://www.etsy.com/uk/shop/WestNinthVintage

Camryn Forrest Designs

Handmade snowglobes.
http://camrynforrest.com

ModVic

ModVic repurposes and infuses modern technology and gadgets and everything cool into period, relevant antiques and salvage objects.
http://modvic.com/

General Steampunk Supplies

Calloch Callay

Vintage housewares, accessories and industrial decor.
https://www.etsy.com/uk/shop/CallochCallay

Cogbots

Handmade cogs in all sizes.
http://www.cogbots.com

Dark Knight Armoury

Harnesses, armour, weapons and LARP items.
http://www.darkknightarmoury.com

Index

A

allergic reactions 21

Art Noveau 13

B

beard and moustache care 114

Bioshock 17

bog wood 13

brooches 51

bustles 16, 18, 115, 117, 118

C

cabochons 33

cameo 13, 16, 32, 33, 35, 36

chains 22

clasps 23

cogs 18, 31, 42, 46, 78, 95, 99, 104, 115, 117

colour wheel 93

comics 16

computer games 16

conventions 16, 18, 85

copper 21

corsets 115, 117

cosplay 16, 18

cravat 101, 103, 106, 109

D

decopunk 12, 13, 114

dieselpunk 12, 14, 114

dreampunk 12

E

eBay 22

Etsy 115

elastic 83, 84, 106

epaulettes 80, 82, 85

F

fabrics 111

fabric paints 115

fascinator 17, 28, 61, 62, 65, 69, 112, 113

feathers 56, 62, 69, 74, 95

footwear 114, 115

G

gloves and gauntlets 75, 76

glues 51, 52, 73, 74

glue gun 52

goggles 78, 79, 113

gothic 14, 16

H

haberdashery 21, 23

hair extensions 113

hairstyles 16, 62, 66, 112, 114

hat boxes 69

harnesses 83, 84, 115, 117, 118

haute couture 14

J

jabot 101, 106, 109

jet 13, 14

jewellery findings 23

L

leather 28, 39, 74, 75, 83, 87, 93, 95, 111, 115, 117

leather cleaning and conditioning 118

lockets 13, 42, 43

M

millinery 61, 62, 69, 87, 112

moodboard 16, 18, 27, 29, 47, 66

mourning jewellery 13, 15, 16, 27

Mori girls 14

N

netting and tulle 118

P

paints 71, 73, 85

pins 51

Pinterest 29

pocket watch 99, 103, 105

polystyrene 62

post apocalyptic 11

plated metals 21, 47

precious metals 21, 47

public liability and product
  insurance 27

Q

Queen Victoria

R

ray guns 18, 36, 37, 72, 85, 87

retrofuturism 11, 113

ribbons 62, 63

rings 51

romanticism 15, 27

S

safety chain 23

semi precious stones 14, 47

sewing techniques 73, 75, 80, 83

sillica gel 117

small business 27

spats and gaiters 115

spiritualism 15

standard necklace chain 24, 31

sterling silver 21

storage trays 23

T

temporary hair colours 114

tools 19, 22

toolkit 22, 23

top hats 16, 61, 78, 95, 98, 99, 101

trading laws 27

tubular crinoline 87

U

upcycling 18, 111

V

varnish 21

Verne, Jules 16

Victorian jewellery 13, 15, 23, 32, 42

W

Wells, H.G. 16

Y

YouTube 17

Related Titles from Crowood

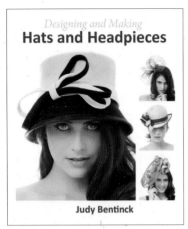

Designing and Making
Hats and Headpieces

Judy Bentinck

ISBN: 978 1 84797 822 6

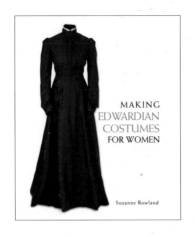

MAKING
EDWARDIAN
COSTUMES
FOR WOMEN

Suzanne Rowland

ISBN: 978 1 78500 102 4

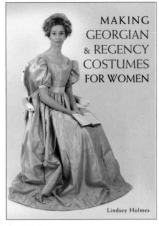

MAKING
GEORGIAN
& REGENCY
COSTUMES
FOR WOMEN

Lindsey Holmes

ISBN: 978 1 78500 070 6

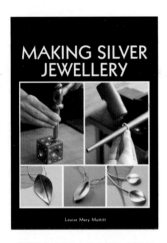

MAKING SILVER
JEWELLERY

Louise Mary Muttitt

ISBN: 978 1 84797 683 3

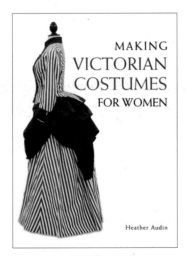

MAKING
VICTORIAN
COSTUMES
FOR WOMEN

Heather Audin

ISBN: 978 1 78500 051 5

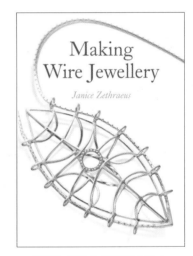

Making
Wire Jewellery

Janice Zethraeus

ISBN: 978 1 78500 165 9

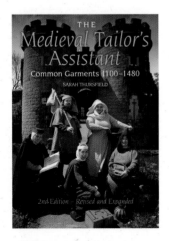

THE
**Medieval Tailor's
Assistant**
Common Garments 1100–1480
SARAH THURSFIELD

2nd Edition – Revised and Expanded

ISBN: 978 1 84797 834 9

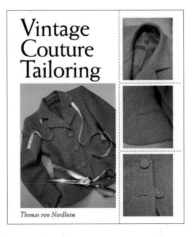

Vintage
Couture
Tailoring

Thomas von Nordheim

ISBN: 978 1 84797 373 3

Vintage Hair Styles
of the 1940s

A Practical Guide

Bethany
Jane
Davies

ISBN: 978 1 84797 832 5